The
Architect's
Apprentice

The Architect's Apprentice

The Story of the Design and Construction of a Wooden Sailboat

Gary M. Schwarzman

SHERIDAN HOUSE

First published 1998 by
Sheridan House Inc.
145 Palisade Street
Dobbs Ferry, NY 10522

Cover photo by Tom Mignone

While all reasonable care has been taken in the publication
of this book, the publisher takes no responsibility for the use
of the methods or products described in this book.

Library of Congress Cataloging-in-Publication Data

Schwarzman, Gary M., 1944–
    The architect's apprentice : the story of the design and
construction of a wooden sailboat / Gary M. Schwarzman.
            p.   cm.
    Includes index.
    ISBN 1-57409-008-9 (alk. paper)
    1. Boatbuilding.   I. Title.
    VM321.S4116   1998
    623.8'1223—dc21   97-46608
                                                                       CIP

Production: Lorretta Palagi
Design: Jill Matthews
Composition: Kate Weisel

Printed in the United States of America

ISBN 1-57409-008-9

Contents

Thanks

For the boat...

To Chuck Paine, Mark Fitzgerald, and Maura Rogers, who comprised the entire staff of C. W. Paine Yacht Design, Inc. To Damian McLaughlin, Nat Bryant, Hugh Popenoe, Rob Robinson, and Mike McGowan, who are mentioned in the text. Also to the folks at Damian's shop who are not mentioned, including Duane Chase, whose craftsmanship receives its deserved expression in his exquisite furniture, and Karen Amorim, who corralled mountains of stray paper into orderly project accounts.

For the book...

To Monica Hough, an outsider to boats and a fine writer herself, for reading my first hesitant chapters and telling me the book was worth writing. To all the members of my own family who labored carefully through stages of the manuscript and offered hundreds of excellent suggestions, both general and specific.

For the experience and the education...

To all of the above, and to Beth.

Houses are but badly built boats so firmly aground that you cannot think of moving them. They are definitely inferior things, belonging to the vegetable not the animal world, rooted and stationary, incapable of gay transition. I admit, doubtfully, as exceptions, snailshells and caravans. The desire to build a house is the tired wish of a man content thenceforward with a single anchorage. The desire to build a boat is the desire of youth, unwilling yet to accept the idea of a final resting place.

It is for that reason, perhaps, that, when it comes, the desire to build a boat is one of those that cannot be resisted. It begins as a little cloud on a serene horizon. It ends by covering the whole sky, so that you can think of nothing else. You must build to regain your freedom. And always you comfort yourself with the thought that yours will be the perfect boat, the boat that you may search the harbors of the world for and not find.

Arthur Ransome
1923

ANASAZI

Length: 42 feet, 9 inches
Displacement: 30,000 pounds
Year Launched: 1993

1

Old Boats and New Boats

This was the first squall that had wind in it. We were sailing along the northern coast of Brazil, across the mouth of the Amazon River, toward French Guiana.

The boat was *Bantry Bay*, the wooden sailing cutter we'd learned to love over the fifteen years we'd sailed her. She was an old double-ender with a tall mast of varnished spruce, her hull painted a light gray. Designed for ocean sailing, she was sturdily built in the 1930s. We had worked hard to get her in shape for our offshore trip, and she had taken us across the North Atlantic, easily weathering a severe gale that had her crew wishing for a night in a motel.

Now she was in the tropical South Atlantic. The wind was light as is typical for the doldrums, the band of unsettled weather that encircles the earth near the equator. The day had brought a succession of squalls. We saw each one first as a dark cloud in the distance. As the cloud came closer, the squall would either hit us or miss and pass by. If it hit, the sky opened up and poured rain.

With the approach of each squall we took in the big light-air sails. With each squall's passing we spread the sails again. It was a pattern, and the pattern seemed to be that the squalls were dark and wet, but they didn't bring high winds.

Lazy, I let myself be sucked in. "They don't seem to have wind in them. This time we'll leave the sails up." And this time, as the squall hit, so did the wind. *Bantry Bay* went over on her ear, not dangerously, but she was momentarily out of control. Steer up into the wind, all hands on deck, and get those sails down. There, that's better.

Bantry Bay was working toward the end of a year's voyage. My wife, Beth, and I had left New England the previous June with our two daughters, Caitlin and Megan, thirteen and twelve years old, respectively, when we set sail. We had sailed across the Atlantic to the Azores, 700 miles from the coast of Portugal, then on to Madeira, the Canary Islands, Senegal, and back across the Atlantic to Brazil. For most of the trip the 43-foot cutter had a crew of five: the two girls, Beth, and me, with the fifth berth occupied by one friend or another who joined us for each major leg.

It had been a good family cruise, beginning with a delicate negotiation over the girls' dreaded separation from classmates and how to keep up with schoolwork. Then there was a great send-off from friends and a stormy but satisfying crossing of the North Atlantic. We gamely stumbled through the Portuguese, Spanish, and French languages. We helped an Azorean fisherman with his nets, became close friends with a French sailing family, and hiked through remote African villages. The girls, in addition to their lessons, learned to stand watch and do celestial navigation. Caitlin turned fourteen on the day we first dropped anchor in the Azores. Megan turned thirteen on a sunny day at sea as we crossed the equator.

Now, having spent four weeks in Brazil, we were headed for Cayenne in French Guiana. From there we planned to cruise through the islands of the eastern Caribbean, then Bermuda, then home.

There was only one impediment. As *Bantry Bay* worked her way westward along Brazil's north coast, we realized that the knockdown in the squall had opened up her planking. Deep in the hull, water was squirting in through open seams. We were in danger of sinking.

The South American coast in that area offers little refuge. In fact, it hardly offers a coast. How could there be a coast, when there is no land? The shore, such as it is, consists of mangrove swamps gradually sloping off into the sea, which is only a few feet deep for miles out. There are no harbors. There are no cities, towns, villages, or roads. Exactly where the land ends and the sea begins is a matter of opinion.

So taking the leaking boat toward shore was not an attractive option. We pumped with hand pumps and electric pumps. We repaired pumps. Heads down in the bilge, we slathered goop into the seams and tacked sheet lead over every leak that could be reached. We sailed for another four days to French Guiana, pumping for a part of every hour of the day and night. At last *Bantry Bay* rested with her anchor set in the muddy bed of the Cayenne River. Without the constant motion of the sea, her leaks slowed.

The town of Cayenne is the home of a large shrimp fleet, and we were able to arrange for the marine railway that serves the shrimp boats to haul *Bantry Bay* out of the water for repairs. We reinforced the planking with blocks and screws, glued wooden wedges into the butt joints, and caulked yards of seams. Afloat again, we sailed to the famous Îles du Salut, the former French prison islands, now a park and low-key tourist attraction.

We rowed ashore, strolled about, gawked at the old prison buildings, and chased the agouti (a raccoon-like animal that has taken over the islands). We rested, sitting on the ground in a grove of palm trees. We hacked the husk off a coconut and cracked it open for a snack. The boat's leaks were stopped; the emergency was over. It was time to talk.

We knew our repairs were sound, but they were not permanent. *Bantry Bay*, fifty years old, had shown her age. In working northwesterly to Cayenne we had left the doldrums and reentered the trade winds, so the sail to the Caribbean would be gentle. The passage to Bermuda was out—too great a possibility of more heavy weather to strain her hull. We would follow the most conservative route home, through the Bahamas and up the Intracoastal Waterway of the United States.

And then what? We could make *Bantry Bay*'s repairs permanent and reinforce her hull (and we subsequently did both), but we would never again feel we could rely on her in heavy weather. She had been ours for a third of her fifty years. She had kept us out of trouble when we didn't deserve it, and she had taught us everything we knew about voyaging by boat. Our daughters had no memory of life without the boat. We had put blood, sweat, and borrowed money into her, and she had given us years of uncommon experiences in fascinating places—Mexico, Costa Rica, Panama, Colombia, Haiti, and Nova Scotia, to name a few. Now, though, it was time for a new boat.

I have always liked change. I am the only person I know who actually enjoys the process of moving. One of my favorite events follows the last performance of a theatrical production, when the scenery is struck to make room for the next show, and in a few hours every sign is erased of the intense work of the previous weeks and months. Gone. Out with the old to make way for the new. Likewise, I have made myself unpopular with seagoing friends by refusing to support the preservation of historic old sailing vessels beyond their useful years. I believe that ships are inherently temporary, and trying to make one permanent is a betrayal of its nature.

So, as much as I loved the old boat, I was not depressed. We would use her well for the remainder of our cruise, but the time had come to look beyond *Bantry Bay*. Although she was yet nameless, *Anasazi* was conceived that day on the Îles du Salut.

⚓

The trip from French Guiana to the island of Tobago was a comfortable four-day sail downwind in the reliable trade winds. Thus we reached the Caribbean and some of the most pleasant cruising in the world. The early summer weather is gentle, and the sailing is easy. Navigation is duck soup: You just sail away from one island and pretty soon you see the next one. The area is well charted, and if that isn't enough then there are guide books to lead the sailor through this well-traveled paradise. After the real challenges of the African and South American coasts, the Caribbean felt like a holiday.

We abandoned our image of ourselves as intrepid travelers and became tourists. On Grenada we watched cacao being processed into chocolate and toured a nutmeg factory. On Bequia a teenage girl visited the boat and showed us how her mother cooked breadfruit. We swam from the beaches and shopped in the markets, and each sundown was greeted with the Caribbean's great bargains: local rum and the juice of the key lime.

Taking advantage of the proximity to the United States, we invited friends and relatives to visit. We enticed Beth's mother and my father each to cruise with us for a week by dangling their granddaughters like lures. The grandparents were rewarded by the satisfaction of receiving lessons in nautical skills from their capable progeny. My brother and his wife spent a pleasant week on board while their toddler learned to climb the companionway ladder. Old friends from California joined our sail up the island chain.

The best event was the one the girls had been waiting for impatiently since we had planned it the previous autumn: Five of their schoolmates, together with a science teacher, flew from Boston to Martinique for a week of education in exotic climes. Each day was mapped out. We splashed through a mangrove swamp. We snorkeled on a windward reef and a leeward reef. We climbed a volcano and trudged through a rain forest. Each day's adventure yielded samples for the microscope and observations for the lab notebook. Somehow there was still time to send the kids off to practice their French by shopping for groceries in the open market, each with his or her assigned purchase. The week ended with dinner in a Real French Restaurant and homemade awards for everyone, some for rather unlikely accomplishments.

In all this activity our schedule went by the boards, and we found ourselves looking at long-established professional commitments but no time to get home to meet them. So it was that Beth flew from Antigua to Utah to serve as geological guide on a Grand Canyon trip, and a few days later Caitlin, Megan, and I flew to California to allow me to begin a summer of business activity. We arranged for some fellow cruisers to take *Bantry Bay* on the long trip to Florida and then home to New England.

By summer's end we had bought a Toyota mini-van and drove across North America. We reclaimed our house and resumed normal small town life. The girls' high school years included some of the usual difficulties that beset teenagers, but they were also marked by a level of confidence and maturity that naturally results from having taken true responsibility on an ocean-going sailing vessel. They soon became student leaders.

We had taken our Atlantic cruise as late in the kids' adolescence as possible. Now it played a big part in their lives, at least to judge by its prominence in each of their college application essays. Then again, perhaps they simply recognized the value of appearing a bit exotic.

⚓

As planned, we put *Bantry Bay* up for sale. The market for old wooden boats, never exactly a hotbed of speculative excess, was going through a particularly slow phase. We were in no hurry, though, and we simply continued to use the boat as usual. We made the bottom repairs more permanent. We cruised the bays and islands of the Maine coast as vacations permitted.

Two years went by with occasional communication from the broker but barely a nibble of interest. Then a prospective buyer made an appointment to see *Bantry Bay*. We cleaned her up a bit, and I waited at the dock to row buyer and broker out to the mooring.

When they arrived I hoped I was looking at the wrong person. The prospective buyer was an obese, middle-aged man, accompanied by a younger man whose connection to the process remained mysterious. It seemed that they were searching for a way to live on the water at very little expense. Well, at the price we were asking for the old boat, they had the expense part right.

I shepherded the group into the dinghy and managed to get each person seated. I rowed, very carefully, toward *Bantry Bay*. We arrived without mishap. With some difficulty and awkwardness, Mr. Buyer clambered aboard.

They looked over the boat and asked irrelevant questions. It was obvious that they didn't know what they were getting into and were not inclined to learn. I had visions of the future: They would move aboard and totally neglect the boat. The boat would deteriorate—grass growing around the waterline, peeling paint exposing weathered wood. The abuse would accumulate until a hose broke or the worms ate through, and one day she would sink at her mooring.

The tour of inspection finally ended. I rowed the group back to the dock, and we parted. I hoped and trusted that would be the end of it, but two days later we received an offer not far below our asking price.

It is possible to betray someone to whom you are expected to be loyal—a boss, a lover, a political leader. I find it much harder to imagine betraying someone who has taught you important things. The act of teaching and the process of learning create a strong obligation of loyalty. In our nineteen years together *Bantry Bay* had been many things to us, but for all of that time she had been our teacher. I wanted to sell the boat, but I couldn't consign her to end her days as a neglected barge. With apologies to the broker, I didn't respond to the offer.

Within a few weeks another buyer appeared. He arrived one morning in his pickup truck after driving down from Maine. There was nothing yachty about Fred, a former chemical engineer who had turned to house construction. I gathered that some domestic upheaval had occurred in his life; now he was looking for a boat to spend some time on sailing locally with his young son.

Fred had once built a boat himself. As he looked *Bantry Bay* over, the beam of his flashlight stopped in the right places: the stem, the heels of the frames. This man knew how to inspect an old boat. He wasn't expecting perfection and didn't find it, but he liked the simple, heavy construction.

Fred's offer was low, but it wasn't absurd. There were a few weeks of counteroffers, pulling the money together, and an inspection by a marine surveyor, but Fred wanted to buy the boat and we wanted to sell it to him, so *Bantry Bay* had found her new owner.

By now it was January, and *Bantry Bay* was secured to a dock for the winter, plumbing drained, and engine laid up. Beth and I volunteered to continue to look after her until the spring weather permitted Fred to take her home. In March Fred drove down to spend some time aboard getting her ready for the trip.

We had already prepared a long list of "Things the New Owner Should Know" about *Bantry Bay*'s history, construction, and condition. Beth readily supplemented the list. "Always turn the propane valve off after using the stove. We leave the key in the valve to show that it's on. Then before lighting the stove I always check that the knobs on the stove top are off. Also, we turn the main battery switch off when we leave the boat, just in case."

Fred interrupted her with a smile. "Wait a minute. I'm not sure if I bought this boat, or I'm just renting it." He had a point. Our proprietary feelings about *Bantry Bay*, and the corresponding sense of responsibility for her welfare, had grown over a nineteen-year intimate association. Signing a bill of sale and cashing a check hadn't changed our attitude toward her one bit.

Out of respect for the difficulty of handling *Bantry Bay* under power in tight places, Fred accepted my offer to pilot her through the narrow opening of the Woods Hole drawbridge. I left the wheel for the last time, and Fred guided her to her mooring in the outer harbor. With a friend joining him as crew, he would leave the next morning to catch a favorable current through the Cape Cod Canal.

At 7:00 A.M. Beth and I drove to the harbor. Out of sight behind bushes on the shore, we watched *Bantry Bay*'s new owner working on deck. Then, without anyone asking our permission, her new crew slipped her mooring and motored out of the harbor into the Woods Hole passage. It was the first time in nineteen years that I had stood on shore and watched my boat going away. Beth cried. Despite my vaunted love of change, I was sentimental and sad.

⚓

My own sailing career began in my teens when my father, in partnership with a friend, purchased what might most charitably be called an "entry-level sailboat." The Snark consisted of a bathtub-like hull of molded Styrofoam fitted out with a sporty yellow plastic sail. We slathered the hull with fiberglass and epoxy resin to protect the soft Styrofoam. As the resin cured, we read a book on how to sail.

The book must have contained a few inaccuracies, because instead of sailing smoothly in all directions as the diagrams indicated, we spent most of our time sitting in several gallons of lake water while being flogged about the head and shoulders with yellow plastic. Only gradually did we each learn to make the boat do most of what we intended at least some of the time. The book started to make better sense, too.

Dad moved up to a small racing boat and joined a local sailing club. We entered races on Wednesday evenings and Sunday afternoons. Our particular contribution to the races was providing a "rest of the fleet" for the winners to lead, but we did pick up some more sailing knowledge. By now at least we could control the boat comfortably.

Beth's principal childhood exposure to boats (not counting her attempts to water-ski with her sisters behind a 3-horsepower outboard) was the family canoe. Always inventive, her father equipped the canoe with homemade sailing gear for which her mother sewed a sail from a war-surplus parachute. The rig worked pretty well downwind. Upwind, well, that's what the paddles were for. This navigational strategy has been practiced successfully since the days when Roman galley slaves prayed for fair winds.

Beth and I met in college in Minnesota. Despite the ostensible proximity of 10,000 lakes, we didn't sail there at all. We were probably too busy studying. A year or two after college we were both living in the San Francisco Bay area, and occasionally we would rent a small sailboat together for an afternoon's recreation. Still, sailing was a very incidental activity.

Not long after we were married, my father invited Beth and me to join him and some friends on a chartered sailboat in the Virgin Islands. We newlyweds were the junior members of the crew of six aboard a 35-footer. With little experience but plenty of enthusiasm we tried to learn every task from setting the anchor to cajoling the engine.

The Caribbean worked its magic. Exhilarating passages, foreign ports, white beaches, turquoise bays, and the parade of graceful boats from all over the globe—we wanted to see more of this world. It wasn't just the sailing; the idea of cruising to out-of-the-way spots with your house on your back seemed just the thing to do.

We returned to reality, urban sprawl, and our daily jobs. It was another year before we actually decided to buy a boat. Then we searched the California coast for something big enough for cruising but small enough to afford. Most people in that circumstance would find a nice used 27-footer, inexpensive enough, no great maintenance problem, suitable for weekends on the bay and the occasional vacation cruise. Somehow in Long Beach we found *Bantry Bay*, a 43-foot, 20-ton relic of 1930s yachting. Her survey report pronounced her "of good appearance and design" but in need of some two dozen repairs—everything from rusted fittings to rot in planks—that I didn't have a clue how to make. As a first boat it was a completely ridiculous choice—and we have never regretted it.

Buying *Bantry Bay* required finding a bank with a loan officer who knew nothing about boats and was willing to accept my explanations and show of confidence. Eventually that and the other obstacles were overcome, the papers were signed, and Beth phoned her parents with the news: We had bought a 43-foot boat, and we were expecting our first child.

⚓

The boat was a fixture in the lives of our small daughters as we spent weekends sailing San Francisco Bay. The main boom supported their swings. They crawled, then toddled, with their harnesses always tethered to a strong point. They took their naps in hammocks slung across the cabin.

With the energy of youth and the help of all the friends we could recruit, Beth and I learned to handle the big old boat. We also tackled her problems. The gentle life in southern California had let her go soft. Every time we sailed, another fitting would break. We discovered frames with rot and keel bolts that were hanging on by rusty threads instead of inch-thick steel. Fixing her faults required knowledge and skills we didn't have. We read books; we asked everyone's advice; we hired old shipwrights; we made innumerable mistakes.

Somehow *Bantry Bay* forgave our blissful ignorance, misguided efforts, and blind neglect, and she taught us. Over the next few years we slowly repaired most of her problems while we paid off the bank. As we gained confidence and equity, we also started thinking about why we owned a 43-foot boat, anyway. It was time to start planning a first real cruise.

⚓

It wasn't hard to shape an interesting itinerary: a trip down the Pacific coast of Mexico and Central America, the Panama Canal, then the islands of the Caribbean. That should take almost a year, and there was no point in trying to plan any further than that. Beth's sister, Laurel, and Laurel's boyfriend, Dick, agreed to join us in the venture.

First we needed to get the boat ready, and the four of us poured ourselves into the hard work. We installed a self-steering device, drove new keel bolts, built shelves and storage lockers, sealed leaky hatches, and completed a hundred other jobs. The workmanship wouldn't have impressed the lowest shipyard apprentice, but it was safe and practical. A pair of vice grip pliers sufficed to keep the propeller shaft from turning while we were sailing. The old enameled steel cooking stove should have been replaced, but we made do with an overhaul. We supplemented our sail inventory with some used bargains.

The lists—the interminable, tyrannical, ever-growing lists—finally lost out to the advance of the seasons. We had to be out of northern California before the winter storms. Ruthlessly, we postponed every job that was in any way optional. As our October departure date approached, the boat floated lower under the weight of the bags of groceries that had twice filled Dick's pickup truck. We left the dock with the farewell waves and good wishes of friends and family and headed up San Francisco Bay. As soon as the dock was out of sight, we went back to stowing groceries.

So far, voyaging by sail had been an image. How would reality compare? We had been eager audiences to dockside yarn spinners, and we had read extensively of others' experiences, both in narrative accounts and in magazine articles on safety at sea, preserving food, anchoring techniques, and all the rest. We had studied the excellent books of encyclopedic scope by Eric Hiscock and Donald Street that provide technical details of everything from sailboat rigging and route planning through celestial navigation and the formalities of customs and immigration procedures. Gradually an image coalesced from the experiences of others, and we had made our plans and decisions accordingly. How well would that image serve our own experience?

It wasn't long before we began to test the image. After sailing from our dock south of San Francisco, we arrived after dark in a protected cove just inside the Golden Gate, dropped anchor, and retired to our bunks while awaiting a favorable tide. We were determined to be True Sailors, waiting for wind and tide if necessary, but in harmony with the Forces of Nature. Waking after midnight we got under way and sailed on a gentle wind under a starry sky out the Golden Gate, San Francisco Bay's portal to the Pacific. We passed Mile Rock and then Point Lobos and made the big left turn to the south: We were on our way to the tropics.

An hour later the wind died completely, and the only remaining Force of Nature was the ocean swell that rolled

Bantry Bay maddeningly from side to side, sails slatting uselessly, running rigging slamming back and forth. Sleep was impossible; we were going nowhere. We remained True Sailors, although of course we were not exactly sailing, until dawn. Still no wind. Bleary-eyed, we decided that getting to Monterey sounded better than being True Sailors. We started up the diesel.

⚓

It is possible to have interesting experiences by design and plan, but it seems more common to have them by circumstance: If you put yourself in a position in which interesting experiences can happen, they probably will.

Sailing down the Pacific coast of North America in a 40-year-old wooden boat with two children then five and three years of age was not unduly dangerous and not even remarkably difficult, but it was an opportunity for interesting experiences. We had our share, and, without our being particularly conscious of it, we gradually learned from them. So did the kids. Some months later, as we tied *Bantry Bay* to a dock in Costa Rica, an American client of a local sport fishing boat struck up a friendly conversation with our sophisticated five-year-old. When he was finished asking questions she turned to Beth in amazement, "Mommy, that man doesn't know anything about boats!"

Our image of voyaging and of ourselves as cruising sailors, initially based on reading and imagination, gradually changed as we gained our own experience. From the day-to-day incidents of living aboard and sailing, from our minor successes and minor catastrophes, we became more knowledgeable and more opinionated on matters of boat design, construction, and outfitting. All of these thoughts would later generate the concepts for the design of *Anasazi*. If such a collection of experiences and opinions can be called a philosophy, then we developed a cruising philosophy.

One of the key characteristics of anybody's cruising philosophy is where technology falls on a given scale from simplicity to gadgetry. This issue often provokes arguments about "convenience," but that doesn't help at all. For one person, convenience means pressure water in the sink when you turn on the tap. Other folks find it inconvenient to provide the space, maintenance, and electrical power that pressurized water requires, convinced they get just as much water, more reliably and at less cost, by tapping a foot pump while washing dishes under the sink spout. Their friends on the next boat think all that pumping and plumbing is a nuisance; they'll wash dishes in a bucket on deck and feel that their life is easier for it.

Everyone wants as much simplicity as his or her own need for convenience will permit. Beth is better at finding that simplicity than I am, always adapting to avoid gadgets. She refuses to have a refrigerator, or even an icebox, on board because she finds them inconvenient and would rather plan menus around food that doesn't need refrigeration.

Here's another example of the simplicity scale. On a sailboat one often needs to attach a rope to a pole, and there are three ways to accomplish this feat, in order of simplicity:

1. Attach a piece of hardware to the pole, and attach the rope to the hardware.
2. Pass the rope through a hole in the pole.
3. Wrap the rope around and around the pole.

The more experience you have, the better you become at avoiding the first method and using the latter two. As the Shakers knew, simplicity is a habit that takes learning.

Does this sound like we're a couple of eccentrics? Are we self-denying, back-to-nature, Thoreau worshippers? Well, Beth is vice chair of the Board of Trustees of the local private school, and my career has been in commercial computer software. We have a home computer and a fax machine. We read financial reports and take business trips. We watch NFL football on Sunday.

⚓

With our very own cruising philosophy adding to the weight on board, our first cruise continued through the Panama Canal and the San Blas Islands, to Colombia, Jamaica, Haiti, and the Bahamas. Our grocery supply and our bank account diminished. Our children grew. On a balmy day in July we reentered the United States at Morehead City, North Carolina. By late autumn we had left *Bantry Bay* in the care of a family in Massachusetts, and we were driving across country, home to California.

Three years later, having sold our house in San Francisco, we were back on the road with all of our household possessions, leaving California to settle in New England. My business kept me traveling, Beth established herself in the world of science education, and the girls' schooling changed from urban to small town. We sailed in the summertime as our schedules permitted.

As the girls entered adolescence, the center of their interests naturally began to shift away from family and toward school and friends. If we were going to tear them away for one more major family cruise, we'd better do it soon.

Once again we poured ourselves into months of plans and preparations. On a sunny day in June, at the age of fifty-one, *Bantry Bay* began her circuit of the North Atlantic Ocean. The following spring, while she was anchored off the Îles du Salut, we decided to design and build *Anasazi*.

2

Design

The accounts of the British yachtsmen of the 1930s, 40s, and 50s convey a pleasant impression of the process of yacht design. The prospective owner brings to a naval architect of renown his entire statement of requirements, effortlessly distilled to a few expressive phrases: "A sound cruising vessel, but capable of a turn of speed, suitable to nip around Cape Horn before sailing the Bering Sea." The naval architect asks a few pithy questions, implying a wealth of detail that need not be mentioned. Correspondence ensues in which questions are asked and answered with a degree of reflection appropriate to the pace of the mails. The resulting design is built, and the owner sails into the sunset.

Of course, no one actually believes that, right? I certainly knew better. But there is that image of a deep meeting of minds in composed discourse, preferably while drawing on a good pipe, that is alluring. If I didn't believe it, neither did I thoroughly reject the picture.

To start, then, we would need a statement of requirements. I wrote one. It started with a declaration of design objectives:

1. This boat must be beautiful. The blood, sweat, and tears that go into a boat must be justified by something, and one of the best justifications is the pleasure of looking at her. But what is beautiful? To us a number of the Alden designs are close to the ideal: a spoon bow, graceful sheer, an oval transom, with moderate rake to the mast.

2. She must be strong and seaworthy. That's one important reason for the wood laminate construction. Although a circumnavigation is not on the agenda, offshore cruising is.

3. Comfort is high on the list of objectives. She should have a comfortable motion under way and provide for comfortable accommodations above and below decks, at sea and at anchor.

4. She must sail well. Although she won't set any speed records, a good design should be reasonably fast, weatherly, and handy. We'd expect her to tack in 90 degrees true.

5. She must be built at a relatively low cost. While we won't compromise basic seaworthiness, we can work for low cost in many areas. We are great scroungers of used materials and equipment. And we cheerfully live without pressure water, radar, refrigeration, teak cabinetry, a generator, and lots of similar luxuries. Most of the sails will be purchased used. Although the boat will basically be professionally built, we can do a great deal of the finishing work and fitting out. Where some desirable but expensive feature isn't essential to the completion of the vessel, it may be designed but postponed for owner completion.

Ten pages later the document finally wound down, after describing our expectations as to hull form, construction method, rig, interior arrangements, engine, and several other details. So much for my image of a few expressive phrases.

Having cruised on sailboats over a twenty-year period we had no lack of opinions about the characteristics we wanted in a boat. Writing them down came easily. We even had a fair sense of the trade-off decisions to be made. We incorporated most of our old ideas and invented quite a few new ones. Some of these ideas were actually good. Some sounded sensible but betrayed our innocence. Some were damned foolish.

Writing down all of these opinions allowed us to focus on the project. Another advantage was that it kept Beth and me communicating with each other. If one of us thought this boat was to be a gaff schooner and the other was picturing a ketch with center cockpit, this was a good time to figure that out.

And, of course, it gave the naval architect a place to start. It may also have given him an impression of the people he was dealing with. If that impression was accurate, it wasn't *so* accurate as to dissuade any architect from accepting the job.

The ten pages of design requirements served yet one more purpose—as a tangible object that was the start of our new boat. We could reread it, talk about it, show it to people. It lent a sense of commitment to the project, even though it was nothing but our own words on paper. And therein lay the problem: There was no reality check. No qualified outsider had cast a cold, unbiased eye on our plans and pronounced them possible. Just as the design ideas were coalescing in my mind, I was also becoming aware of the depth of my ignorance of the real world of building boats.

My own business experience is in computer software, fairly complex custom-tailored stuff that is sold to large municipal governments to support public safety. I've worked with outfits like the Baltimore Police Department and the Milwaukee Fire Department. Some of that experience would be helpful—project planning, for example. But now we would be dealing with small boat building businesses run by men

who were fiercely independent, fiercely capable, and fiercely individual. If they had wanted safe, lucrative professions, they'd be somewhere else. I knew that the world of civil service, public procurements, and government bureaucracy was a poor training ground for the business side of boat building.

Fortunately, I found a good way to address my ignorance. Our friend Bob Ackland had made a second career in the yacht business. Most recently, he had been a managing principal in one of Cape Cod's top boatyards, Falmouth Marine Railway. (That glorious name, alas, has now succumbed to the corporate anonymity of "FMR, Inc.") There could be no better person than Bob to ask about the business of building boats.

Bob agreed to meet with us and answered every question we could think of about builders, designers, specifications, and contracts. Patiently and generously he spent most of a morning with us. By the time he left, the opaque blur in my mind had changed to a sequence of clear steps.

Bob mentioned a dozen naval architects and what he knew about each. One was an expert in high-tech materials. One was oriented to heavy boats. One was particularly flexible. We chose two likely-sounding names as a start. We telephoned, sent copies of the design requirements, and set up meetings for successive days with Dieter Empacher and Chuck Paine.

On a sunny February morning Beth and I piled our papers and our checklists into the Toyota mini-van and drove two hours north to Salem. Dieter Empacher's unimposing office occupied part of a frame house near the old Dion boatyard. We arrived early, and Dieter was out. We were directed upstairs to wait.

The office had all the charm we had pictured. Photos and half-models on the walls spoke of past commissions. Reference books and catalogs filled shelves. Drawings of boats—works in progress?—were scattered about. We waited impatiently.

Dieter arrived just before the appointed hour, a man of medium height, medium age, sandy hair, and a strong Germanic accent. After the obligatory opening small talk, he pulled out a rolled drawing. "I just made a quick drawing. Let me show you."

My heart quickened; this was the start of the design! We stood around the drawing board as Dieter quickly spread out the profile view of a 40-foot cutter. My heart sank. This drawing looked like a dozen modern boats I'd seen and was fairly similar to several production models. It had no sense of the old Alden yachts, much less of their fisherman schooner forebears.

But wait. What is design if not a series of refinements based on evolving communication? My ten-page opus notwithstanding, we couldn't expect Dieter to share our values, only to learn them. So we talked.

And as we talked, it became clear that the only information we had succeeded in imparting was the size of the boat and the rig. Once he learned that a cruising sailboat in the form of a 40-foot cutter was wanted, for all practical purposes Dieter had stopped reading. Although he seemed anxious to please on any point we raised, we weren't really communicating; there was no give and take of ideas. We promised to "think about it," shook hands, and left.

The next morning found us admiring the windjammer fleet frozen into the harbor of Camden, Maine, where Chuck Paine's office overlooks the water. Having admired his designs for years, I was feeling a bit awed at the prospect of meeting him. We stepped through the office door, he turned from his drafting table, and we all shook hands.

Chuck Paine is in early middle age. He's a bit shorter than I, and I'm just 5 feet, 8 inches. With his sparkling blue eyes and a salt-and-pepper beard, he can look positively elfin. There's a lot of Maine in Chuck's New England accent, and his speech is sprinkled with the words of naval architecture. A bracing timber is "in way of" the mast when the two are lined up. To move a line slightly on a drawing is to "urge" it.

As we talked about the design it was clear that Chuck had read our requirements, remembered them, and given them some real thought. We talked about some of his early designs, especially *Annie*, a charming 30-foot sloop that everyone loves, Beth and me included. Chuck had owned one of the *Annie*'s himself, and it was one of his favorite boats. We talked about his later work in stock boats and custom designs for large yachts in aluminum and fiber-glass.

Chuck gave us the sense that he not only understood our requirements, but that he shared our values in boats. To some extent, creating that impression is a measure of his skill as a businessman selling his services. I think it also reflects a genuine ability to empathize with his clients and a sincere understanding that the success of his de-signs depends on that ability.

The uncomfortable subject had to be raised. "What will all this cost?"

Chuck's reply was straightforward. "We can work it dif-ferent ways. If you need a fixed price, we can do that, but it removes some flexibility that we probably should retain. What we'd prefer to do is charge by the hour. Our hourly rate is twenty-seven dollars and fifty cents, and we'd ask for a retainer of twenty-five hundred dollars to be applied against the first costs. I can tell you from experience that this boat will come to about twenty thousand dollars for the completed design."

Beth and I excused ourselves and walked outside to cau-cus. We strolled along the planked wharf, warm in the sun-shine, but chilled by the breeze off the cold harbor. No doubt about it, we had fallen in love. Although it was much smaller than our intended boat, we saw in his *Annie* both the shapes and the values of our dream. Here was a well-known, re-spected naval architect who really understood our kind of boat. We seemed to communicate well. His rate was almost ridiculously low (it has since increased to a level that leaves a living wage after the rent's been paid), and the overall cost was about what Bob Ackland had estimated. We delib-erated carefully for, oh, twenty or thirty seconds. We walked back inside and shook hands on the deal. There was never any more contract than that.

⚓

There is that moment that follows any commitment, when you have just agreed to buy the house, or leave your job, or "take this woman to be your . . . ." You know you wanted this. You decided to do it. You're reasonably sure you still want it. But there's that too-familiar hollow feeling inside, and you can't quite banish the thought of "My God, what have I done?"

The five-hour drive home from Camden afforded that thought plenty of opportunity to pry open the door and take up residence. Sometimes we chattered about design details. Sometimes we drove in silence. Sometimes we reassured ourselves. In the end we took refuge in repeating all of the reasons why we had decided to build this boat. We arrived home content.

Although Beth and I were itching to start the design in earnest, Chuck had some competing commitments, so we had scheduled the next meeting for the middle of March, six weeks away. Meanwhile we had some assignments.

We were to sketch a floor plan of the interior of the boat. Chuck suggested this as the best way to communicate our ideas on layout. I was hurrying to the airport for a week's business trip, but I quickly drew the outline of a boat on a blank sheet of paper, added a scale, and made copies for each of us to work on. Beth worked on hers at the kitchen table; I did mine on a tray table somewhere over Nebraska. When we compared notes later, the two sketches were almost identical.

The entrance to the cabin, called the companionway, is from the cockpit, down a steep set of steps. To your immediate left is the head of a berth whose foot extends aft under the cockpit. Forward of that, still on your left, is the chart table, the boat's navigation center, with reference books, plotting instruments, and the radio.

Just beyond the chart table, and still within a step or two of the companionway, is the enclosed head with sink and toilet. On many boats the head is placed all the way forward, but we've been seasick often enough to know better. Enclosed spaces promote *mal de mer*, so we wanted to place the head aft where the motion is least uncomfortable. Besides, when you're making a mad dash below, those few steps can make all the difference.

On your right, opposite all this, is the galley. To the detriment of our waistlines, the pleasures of eating play a rather central role in our life, and we granted the galley a correspondingly central, even commanding position in the boat. At seven feet in length it may be the most spacious galley that has ever fed the crew of a 42-foot sailboat.

Despite the galley's expanse, the width of the floor space between counters is just larger than the width of the cook. This is quite intentional; you want to be able to brace yourself in a seaway while your hands are occupied catching dishes and pots that have gone flying.

The saloon, the boat's living and dining room, occupies the full width of the hull forward of the galley. The saloon's drop-leaf table receives ample support from the mast. Forward of all this, in the bow of the boat, is a sleeping cabin.

With the double berth forward, two settees in the saloon, one upper berth (known as a "pilot berth") in the saloon, and the quarter berth by the companionway, there is comfortable sleeping space for six adults. Sleeping in the forward cabin's double berth, though, will not work well in a heavy sea. A double bed is comfortable as long as it stays still. Without restraints, the occupants will spend all night trying not to be rolled out of bed. The single berths are equipped with canvas bunk boards that are easily tied into position or stowed away when not in use. They hold the sleeper snug and comfortable. Such a convenience is impractical in a double berth, and even if a way to rig it could be devised, the motion in the bow of a boat is always the most violent. So there are six berths, but only four "sea berths."

I've just described the boat that was built. Our first sketch was slightly more optimistic because we tried to use some space that didn't exist. We drew our interior to the largest plan view of the boat, not making enough allowance for space lost as the hull curves inward toward the bottom. But the corrections were small: one berth in the saloon became a single, rather than a pull-out double, and the separate locker for wet-weather gear that we had envisioned by the companionway was eliminated. Those two changes excepted, the layout held unchanged throughout the design process.

A boat show salesman, nattily casual in his topsiders and blue blazer, would chuckle condescendingly at the inadequacies of our interior arrangement. After all, his 42-footer sleeps eight, has two private cabins (which he calls "staterooms"), two heads, and a dressing vanity.

If that were our boat, we'd probably use the second head to store garlic, canned bacon, and powdered buttermilk. We carry four anchors and 1,200 feet of anchor line. We provision to be able to spend three months on the coast of Central America and still have chutney for the curry, cranberry sauce for the chicken, and chocolate chips for the cookies.

We allow a generous amount of space to facilitate maintenance. I can reach every part of the engine—no common ability on a sailboat. We're prepared to replace water hoses, fuel injectors, and rigging cables, and we have the supplies and tools to repair a torn sail, a broken cabin lamp, or a hole in the hull if need be. The tanks hold engine fuel for 150 hours and cooking fuel for three months. All of this concern for provisions and supplies uses cubic footage that our salesman friend might have allocated to the pleasures of condominium living. That's what it takes to sell boats in his market.

This is beginning to sound like the work of a survivalist nut-case. Honest, I'm not. It's just that if you want to cruise beyond the reach of Federal Express, self-reliance is the name of the game. Lose an anchor in Long Island Sound, and you can replace it in a matter of hours. Lose an anchor in the Cape Verde Islands, and the problem becomes more interesting.

So our boat would accommodate four to six people comfortably, with plenty of room for provisions and supplies. We tidied up our drawing and mailed it to Chuck.

⚓

There was never any doubt that our next boat would be made of wood. I could wax polytechnical about wood's strength-to-weight ratio, its resistance to mechanical fatigue, and its insulating qualities. But let's face it, I just like wood. Wooden things are nicer than fiberglass things. When the distinguished yacht designer L. Francis Herreshoff referred to fiberglass as "frozen snot," did anyone disagree with him?

Not counting dugout canoes, all wooden boats were built in roughly the same way for centuries: plank-on-frame. Picture the skeleton of a whale lying on its back. The shape and structure are formed by ribs curving upward from a horizontal backbone. Now nail (or screw) planks along those ribs lengthwise, and you have a plank-on-frame boat. Whether it's a Roman trireme, a Spanish galleon, an English tea clipper, or a Grand Banks fishing schooner, that's how it was built.

The invention of waterproof glue opened up a new possibility: plywood. Far stronger for its weight than ordinary lumber, plywood requires less supporting structure. It also spans more area without joints.

But plywood comes in flat sheets. Although the sheets will take some bend, and some very successful boats have been built of plywood, you can't get plywood to form the compound curves of a conventional hull shape any more than you can use plywood to build a Buick. The solution is to laminate thin, bendable strips of wood into place, side by side and layer by layer, building up the curved shape of the boat. Each strip of wood is glued to its neighbors, with glue between the layers. Because the wood runs in a different direction in each layer the whole structure is tremendously strong. Since the joints in individual layers are overlapped, the surface is continuous and reliably waterproof over the whole boat.

This technique of laminated wood construction has been popularized with remarkable success by Gougeon Brothers, Inc., of Bay City, Michigan. As a boatbuilder and epoxy formulator, Gougeon Brothers has taken the lead in research and engineering in wood-epoxy construction of an amazing variety of boats, not to mention architectural sculpture and rotor blades for helicopters. Gougeon Brothers has taken pains to make its results available and understandable to the boatbuilding trade. As a result, its trademarked WEST System epoxy has become the standard for the industry.

We wanted the new boat to be built of wood, but we also wanted to be able to leave it out of the water for extended periods—years maybe—without damaging it. In a plank-on-frame boat the wood gets wet and expands. Repeated wetting and drying, with parts expanding and contracting, weakens the boat. If you've seen an old wooden hull propped up behind someone's barn and ignored for a few years, then you've seen what I mean. A hull of wood laminate construction is completely encapsulated in epoxy, so in the water or out there should be almost no change in the moisture content of the wood. With reasonable care you can store a wood laminate boat on land for many years without damage.

Finally, we were, well, a little sensitive about leaks. It's an unfair slight to the legions of durable, watertight boats planked by skilled traditional builders, but after having spent days pumping like the frightened fool I was, I just can't help thinking of a plank-on-frame boat as a collection of open seams held together by—what exactly does hold those things together, anyway?

So this boat was to be of laminated wood construction. I said this to Chuck Paine at our first meeting, and his response was quick and unequivocal. "The cheapest method of wood laminate construction is going to be strip planking with diagonal veneers over the strip planks. The strip planks form the shape, so the bulkheads that support the strip planking stay in the boat. You don't need a lot of structure that gets thrown out." And so it was.

⚓

Chuck Paine's design office is filled with light and the glory of past and future boats. Between the activity in constant view across the harbor and the distractions of fascinating books, drawings, and photos in the office, it is hard to stay focused on the drafting tables. The office is a temple to the art of yacht design. There is not a chair in the place, not even a tall stool. The principal pieces of furniture are the drafting tables, and work is accomplished in the standing position. The only visible concession to human comfort is the coffee pot.

Beth and I had betrayed our eagerness by arriving early and prepared. In addition to the work on the accommodation plan we had mailed ahead some sketches and notes for a sail plan. From the beginning, we had decided on a Marconi cutter rig.

The word *Marconi* implies triangular sails, rather than the old four-sided gaff sails. Triangular sails need a taller mast than gaff sails, and the tall mast is supported by guy wires. That type of rig reminded an early observer of a radio antenna, or Marconi station.

I could spend hours exploring the changing definition of the word *cutter,* but I'll spare you all that and just tell you that this rig has a single mast. There's a triangular mainsail behind the mast, and two or more jibs ahead of it. The outermost jib flies from a bowsprit extending from the boat's bow. Anyone who wishes to argue the fine points of that definition may take it up with the bartender at the yacht club.

The cutter rig offers the advantage of a single mast— and, hence, lower cost, less maintenance, and less complexity—while providing some flexibility as to what sails are set for different strengths of wind. The mast is near the center of the boat, so the widest part of the hull is available to anchor the supporting stays, and in heavy weather it is easier to work near the center of the boat than forward.

That's not to say the cutter is the perfect choice. Each of the other rigs (sloop, ketch, schooner, etc.) has its advantages, and all sorts of variants and combinations have been tried. We liked the cutter, though, and Chuck agreed enthusiastically.

He was less enthusiastic about my plan for three jibs. Most cutters these days have a small inner staysail just forward of the mast, then a large genoa jib on the outermost stay. This big outer jib is the workhorse. It helps the boat sail close into the wind, and it is efficient in light and moderate breezes. In strong winds you take the sail in. To do this, many boats today have a furling device that rolls the sail up like a window shade. It's called roller furling, at least when it works. Sometimes it's called roller snarling. While I am not a religious person, I do believe that the existence of roller furling is compelling evidence that Satan is alive and currently resides in a sail loft.

Rather than sell my soul for a window shade, I designed a rig with three small jibs. The three jibs look quite pretty. Dousing the outer one when the wind comes up is quick and easy. Disadvantages? The rig isn't as powerful and efficient as a big genoa, and controlling all three sails gets complicated. Chuck would have predicted all this. Such are the compromises in the designs of boats.

⚓

Chuck reached for a rolled drawing and spread it on his drafting board. Our sketch of the interior had been transformed into an architectural drawing at a scale of 3/4 inch to the foot.

"I've been keeping your interest in visibility in mind. You mentioned being able to see out the portlights." Chuck produced a tape measure and ran it from the floor to Beth's eye-level. "It will be tricky to give you visibility from the galley and still provide good headroom, but I think it's just possible. Furthermore, if the cabin is level, then the forward portlights will be higher."

We worked our way through the drawing. "In wood laminate construction there just isn't enough depth in the hull to situate the engine as far aft as you've drawn it. We need to find a way to place it farther forward, surrounded by cabinetry."

The problem was that the propeller shaft penetrated the hull almost within the cabin area. Obviously if the engine were forward of the propeller shaft it would be in the cabin.

"What about using a V-drive?" I was no expert in this area, but I did have a friend who had kept his engine well aft by turning it end-for-end and placing it aft of—that is, behind—the attachment to the shaft.

"I don't know that I could recommend a V-drive. You don't see them too often, and I'd be concerned about getting parts in the future. Mark, what do you think?"

Mark Fitzgerald is Chuck Paine's chief draftsman. Since this is a small office he's also Chuck's *only* draftsman, or at least the only permanent one. Other design help has been brought in as needed for big projects, but the core of the firm is Chuck and Mark.

In his thirties, Mark is tall and quiet. When he does speak it is softly, as if every sentence were intended to bring calm. Mark says what he thinks.

"Actually, I've been seeing a lot of V-drives. I think we'll be seeing more of them as people try to put more boat in less space. Most of the companies that make transmissions make a V-drive." Mark padded across the carpet in his socks, bent down to a file cabinet and shuffled through some manufacturers' literature.

Mark readily defers to Chuck's considerable experience, sense of aesthetics, and overall feel for boats, but Chuck will often defer to Mark in the area of mechanical systems. It looked like a V-drive would solve our problem.

We talked about the boat's profile. Surely the overall sense of a boat's looks—graceful or awkward, traditional or modern, draft horse or thoroughbred—depends far more on her profile than any other perspective. Here we felt confident: We loved the profile of Alden schooners with their high bow, low sides amidships, and counter stern.

Chuck pulled a blank sheet of paper over his board and swept in some lines. There was the profile of a sailboat, upside down. I was taken aback, but it does make sense: Pivoting your arm at the elbow, your pencil will draw a curve that is concave toward the bottom of the paper, the shape of an upside-down hull. Given some practice, it's the surer way to draw a boat.

We reviewed the basics of the profile and adjusted the drawing: a long keel for steady steering and to protect the propeller and rudder. Chuck wanted the forward edge of the keel to be fairly vertical, rather than gently sloping, to improve sailing performance to windward. We settled the general look of the cabin top and the cockpit. This felt like good progress.

Chuck quizzed us closely on the three headsails. "Tell me why is it you don't want a genoa jib."

I reviewed the reasons: A genoa jib for our boat would come to at least five hundred square feet. Changing sails means stuffing five hundred square feet of recalcitrant Dacron into a sail bag, wrestling the bag down below decks, and setting a working jib in its place. At best, handling that bulky sail is an annoying process and a real storage problem. In my case, the hassle factor means that procrastination sets in. On a sailboat at sea, procrastination comes back to bite you every time.

But the three jibs create a new problem. In general, while a boat is sailing the sails are always on its downwind side. When the boat turns across the wind and there's a new downwind side, the sails are brought from one side of the boat to the other. Trying to accomplish that maneuver with three jibs at once is like trying to handle three fire hoses at once to put out a fire.

The usual solution is to make the innermost jib flop across of its own accord. This is called "self-tacking," and normally requires fitting a spar—which is simply a pole—along the bottom of this inner jib. That spar is a menace. It can flop when you're not expecting it. It is considerably longer and heavier than a baseball bat, and its impact with the skull creates a similar sensation. Even when it's not actively on the rampage, it's an obstacle that adds a threatening aspect to work on the foredeck.

My plan was to make the inner jib capable of self-tacking without using the spar. Since I didn't know how to design a spar-less self-tacking jib, I tried to foist the problem on Chuck. He doubted that it would be possible on this rig, but we tried. (I'm still trying. It doesn't work perfectly, but it works.)

We spent all of one day and part of the next working through different aspects of the design in this fashion. Finally we talked about the overall schedule. This was March.

The preliminary design—hull shape, interior layout, profile, sail plan, and deck plan—together with the specifications, would be complete by about the end of May. We would then stop the progress for a couple of months so that Beth and I could let the design sink in, mull it over, and develop a list of desired changes. By late summer we would be ready to finalize the design and specifications and begin soliciting bids for construction. If we could begin construction in the fall of 1991, we might launch in the late summer of 1992.

No, that's too optimistic. And if it slips a little, even I am not fool enough to try to launch a boat in the middle of a New England winter. So allowing for the time gremlins, launching in the early spring—say, March—of 1993 seemed like a very comfortable plan.

As I write this book, the year 1993 is history, but from our perspective in the spring of 1991, launch day felt like a long two years into the very distant future.

⚓

We set a date to meet again in a few weeks. Meanwhile each of us would work on our parts of the design. We would exchange drawings by mail and fax and discuss them on the telephone.

As the details of the design were filled in, odd differences in our assumptions came to light. As an example consider the bowsprit, the spar that extends ahead of the bow. Its purpose is to support additional sails, but a bowsprit does a lot to determine the look of a traditional sailboat, and the bowsprit we had pictured was similar in proportion to those on the Alden yachts, say 6 or 7 feet long. In the preliminary drawings Chuck had indicated the bowsprit by a stub, without actually showing the whole spar. When the next drawing showed the entire bowsprit, it was only about 30 inches long.

I phoned Chuck. "What happened to the bowsprit? I guess we never discussed it explicitly, but we were assuming a full traditional bowsprit."

"I felt that a long bowsprit is too dangerous at sea. The old timers used to call them 'widow-makers,' you know."

"Gee, we've sailed a lot of miles with a bowsprit. I think a bowsprit needs good footing and lifelines, and there should be a railing at the end, but then the bowsprit becomes a good working platform."

"Are you sure that's what you want? I'm rather reluctant to go ahead with what I think compromises your safety."

"Well, it shouldn't be necessary to work on the bowsprit in really rough weather, because by then you've already taken those sails down. If it does happen, though, I have to admit that we just turn downwind. Then everything stabilizes and working on the bowsprit is much easier, although it's still possible to find yourself waist deep in seawater. Have you done much ocean sailing with a bowsprit?"

"Well, no I haven't, and if that's your opinion and it's what you want, then I'll accept it, but I'd like you to think about it further."

And so it went. When I told the story to my daughter Megan she was puzzled. "Why should a bowsprit be dangerous?" Megan has never known life without a bowsprit. As a small child, all glasses and curly red hair, she played on the bowsprit at anchor, her safety harness clipped to the railing. As a teenager she worked on the bowsprit as a competent member of the crew. It all comes down to what you're accustomed to, I suppose.

We worked over the boat's sheer—the curved profile of the deck line that starts high at the bow, sweeps low amidships, then curves slightly up again to the stern. Modern sailboats tend to have a fairly flat sheer, but a more pronounced sheer (that is, a stronger curve) is characteristic of the traditional designs. Increasing the curve of the sheer provided the added advantage of keeping the outer end of the bowsprit—my "working platform"—that much farther out of the ocean. It took several drawings, but we arrived at a line that pleased everyone.

One day I mentioned to Chuck that we'd see him soon at an upcoming meeting. He hesitated and checked his schedule. "I think we have to reschedule that. Somehow I didn't put it on my calendar, and now I'm committed to be in Florida that week." This was not good news. It seemed that each time we met there was a delay, and the work between meetings had not been proceeding on schedule either. Each delay was small, perhaps a week or two, but the effect was cumulative. And I wasn't certain that the calendar problem was completely inadvertent.

There was nothing to do but concede. Chuck's next available date was in May, another month away, when he planned to be about an hour from our home to visit his mother. It would be pleasant to meet at our house.

⚓

Beth and I have always been drawn to the Southwest. We've hiked and camped in the desert and bounced along the back roads in a Volkswagen. We've pulled cactus thorns from our jeans and bargained for Navajo rugs and jewelry. We've kicked back with a beer and admired the Grand Canyon scenery after rowing Horn Creek Rapid on the Colorado River.

In April we took a week's vacation for a float trip down the San Juan River in southern Utah. It was a comfortable week of camping, rowing, and exploring prehistoric Indian sites in the company of knowledgeable guides. When we returned to our New England lives, the boat had her name.

Anasazi is the name that the Navajo Indians use for the people who were there before them, known now as the fashioners of baskets and pottery and cliff dwellings, but gone from the area before the Navajos arrived. The word appears throughout the Southwest, and for me it conjures up not only those prehistoric people about whom we know very little, but all of the feelings of life in the desert. It translates as *Ancient Enemy*.

We had been casting about for a name, of course. We wanted the name to be unique and to mean something to us. (If you call *Windsong* on the marine radio on a summer weekend in any coastal community in the United States you'll get an average of 17.4 replies. It's a pretty name, but the world doesn't need another *Windsong*.)

The name had to be short—easy to paint on the transom, easy to spell on the radio. The name had to be pronounceable by non-English speakers and readable by most people who read Roman letters. In the office of a Mexican port captain I inflict enough misery with my fractured Spanish while trying to communicate a name like Elisabeth Schwarzman, which to a native Spanish speaker might as well be Sanskrit. At least the boat's name should appear to be rendered in some actual language.

My first impulse was *Anarchist*. Sensibly, Beth vetoed it.

Peter Spectre, who writes on nautical subjects, avers that seven letters in a boat name is good luck, as are three A's.

So *Anasazi* it was. The word conjures up notions of ancestral memories, good thoughts for a boat with strong ties to the fishing schooners that were her forebears. Admittedly, it is not traditional to name a boat after extinct desert dwellers. But the sea *is* an Ancient Enemy, isn't it?

⚓

By now we were pressing ahead with the details of the design. Engaging a professional architect to translate your thoughts and opinions into a coherent design is, admittedly, an exercise in self-indulgence. But it was fun.

We worked in fuel and water tanks with generous capacities. (Chuck convinced us to build the water tanks as part of the hull, which has proved quite successful.) We adjusted the drawings until the cockpit was deep enough for security and comfort, but shallow enough to drain quickly and provide good visibility to a standing helmsman.

When we wanted to reduce the size of the head, Chuck suggested that we construct a mock-up. In our basement we dragged out yardsticks, cardboard, and duct tape and built a model throne room. We took turns climbing inside and pantomimed brushing our teeth and pulling up our pants until we arrived at a practical minimum size.

Each decision was a compromise, an attempt to balance the competing goals of seaworthiness, sailing ability, aesthetics, comfort, and cost. Some items:

- You want to minimize the resistance of the water going by the hull, so the bottom should be flat. But you also want to avoid pounding on choppy seas, so the bottom should be a deep V-shape. Besides, there *will* be some water in the bilge, and a flat bottom means that the water will slosh up into the clothing lockers. So the shape of the bottom is a compromise.

- You want to place the companionway hatch on the boat's centerline because of the importance of keeping that hatch away from the ocean as the sailboat leans over in a strong wind. But you also want room for a spacious galley beside the companionway. So the hatch is moved off-center by just a foot.

- You want room on deck to secure a dinghy behind the mast, but moving the mast a foot farther forward will prevent you from sitting at the cabin table. So the mast is moved six inches, the dinghy space is a bit shorter than hoped, and the table is redrawn.

Virtually every part of the boat was shaped by trade-offs like these. Each person will make each of these decisions differently. There is no Perfect Boat for any of us, but for each person perhaps there is a Perfect Compromise, and that limited, personal goal is the holy grail of the design process.

All of these considerations are Chuck Paine's stock in trade. It was a pleasure to watch Chuck's mind at work, integrating his long experience of cruising boat designs with what he was hearing from us. He always listened carefully, although sometimes he couldn't believe what he heard.

Chuck: "Under this counter I've drawn in a stack of drawers."

Beth: "Oh. We were planning to put the trash bin there, because it's accessible from outside the galley."

Chuck: "All right. We can move the drawers over here by the sink."

Beth:	"Actually, I don't really like a lot of drawers in the kitchen. I'd rather just have the open locker space."
Chuck:	"But a galley needs a stack of drawers."
Beth:	"Well, that's just not my way."

That one was pretty easy. The drawers were conventional but, in Chuck's mind, hardly critical. The icebox was harder.

Beth:	"What does the square on this counter indicate?"
Chuck:	"That's the fridge. We've got full depth here, so it's the best place to situate it."
Beth:	"We're not planning on having a fridge, or any type of icebox."
Chuck:	"But you have to have some kind of icebox."
Beth:	"I'd rather live without it. I think they're more trouble than they're worth. We've cruised for a long time in the tropics without any kind of refrigeration, so I think we know what we're getting into."
Chuck:	"But this is the twentieth century. There just isn't any reason to do without refrigeration. Let's leave it in so you have it to use when you do want it."
Beth:	"No, I don't want to take the space."
Chuck:	"If nothing else, think about resale. Eventually you'll want to sell this boat, and anyone would expect at least an icebox in the galley."
Gary:	"We don't expect to sell this boat for a very long time; that's really not an issue. How about if we just understand that here's a place where we could install an icebox later if we wanted."

Chuck: "Retrofitting an icebox is a hellish job and probably would never be done as well as it should. It's so easy to just build it in during construction."

Beth: "This is *my* galley, and I don't want an icebox."

That ended it. Chuck had put up the good fight, but he ultimately surrendered.

Don't I miss the ability to pull a hamburger out of the fridge and open a cold beer to go with it? Sure I do. Some people wouldn't consider cruising Alaska—much less the Caribbean—without refrigeration. But we've known many experienced sailors besides ourselves who wouldn't have an icebox aboard their boats on a bet. To have cold food you become a slave either to hauling ice or to supplying energy and maintenance to your mechanical refrigerator. Our own choice is to keep it simple. For more detail on the refrigeration choice, see the Appendix. For now, suffice it to say that I've never had reason to complain about the food on *Anasazi.*

⚓

Only after there is fair agreement on the interior arrangement and the overall size and profile of the boat does the architect try to establish the boat's shape accurately.

A naval architect renders the shape of a boat on paper as a series of outlines—slices through the hull in three differ- ent dimensions. The shape of a loaf of bread also can be drawn in this way.

First, slice the loaf in the usual way, and look at the slices. If all of the slices are squarish and of similar size, it's a loaf of Wonder Bread. If the middle slices are oval and the end slices are small and round, it is a long French loaf. It is only necessary to pick a suitable thickness for the slices and show the outline of each slice. Given such a series of outlines, it would be possible to create a model of the loaf, correct in size and proportion. On the naval architect's draw- ing, those slice outlines are called sections.

It is possible, however, to slice that loaf in other ways. With the flat of the blade held horizontal, cut the top off the loaf. Then make another horizontal slice a half-inch lower, and so forth. The outlines of those flat, horizontal slices are called waterlines. Depending on how high or low the loaf (or boat) is floating, one or another of those outlines will indeed be the waterline where it floats.

Finally, turn the knife back to the usual slicing position, but cut the loaf lengthwise, making long vertical slices. The outlines of these slices present yet another view of the loaf's shape. These lines are called the buttocks. No, I don't know why.

The three sets of outlines of the slices—they're contour lines, really—show the same loaf. Although any one set would be sufficient to define the hull's shape, the naval architect uses all three because certain aspects of the shape are more apparent in one perspective than in another. Ultimately the boatbuilder will make use of all three.

In these modern times, computers provide a lot of help in drawing and redrawing these lines. Chuck used the computer to produce a preliminary shape. At that point, however, the experienced eye took over.

"Most of the design software that's used for boats was first developed to design cars. The program we use does a good job of producing fair curves through the middle of the boat, but it doesn't handle the ends as well as we like. So we take the lines off the computer and complete them by hand."

To an experienced mountain hiker the contour lines on a topographic map provide a practical description of a planned hike, but they also elicit visions of broad meadows, tumbling streams, and skyline ridges. Likewise, the sheet of contour maps of the hull—the "lines drawing"—conveys the design better than any picture. An expert will examine the lines drawing and form opinions as to the boat's stability, speed, comfort, and windward ability. The lines also convey an overall sense of the boat's shape, and the beauty of that shape is discernible even to the amateur.

The Canadian dime bears the likeness of the Nova Scotia schooner *Bluenose*. The lines drawing of *Bluenose*, which is sold to tourists in Halifax, is as beautiful a piece of graphic art as I have ever seen.

⚓

To steer a sailboat, you use one of two devices: a tiller or a steering wheel. The tiller is the simpler of the two; it is a handle attached directly to the top of the boat's rudder and is used on all small boats and on some bigger ones up to the 40-foot range. Just grab the tiller and move it, and you are moving the rudder and steering the boat.

Larger, heavier boats need more force than a person can comfortably apply to a tiller; these boats have steering wheels. The steering wheel is attached to the rudder by a mechanical linkage that provides leverage. *Anasazi* would have a steering wheel. But how should it be attached to the rudder?

Again, there are two common choices for steering linkage: rigid, mechanical stuff like gears, or flexible stuff like steel cable and pulleys. The flexible cable has all the advantages of, well, flexibility, but it does have a bit of an image problem. When you hear about failures in steering systems, they are almost entirely failures of the flexible cable. Losing your steering while sailing along a coast is one of those problems that tends to lead to other problems in a hurry.

Chuck described the different types of cable systems and explained that, properly engineered, they could be almost perfectly reliable. But my prejudice had already been formed by those horror stories of the failures of cable steering. Furthermore, I knew that *Bantry Bay*'s old Edson mechanical steering gear was fifty-five years old when we sold the boat, worked perfectly, and probably would have outlived a dozen hulls.

It was considerably easier to decide on a steering gear in concept than to locate one in bronze. The problem was made more difficult by the need to accommodate the sharp angle between the steering wheel and *Anasazi*'s rudder post. The Edson company didn't offer a model that quite fit, but we found a promising candidate in a catalog from the

Lunenburg Foundry in Nova Scotia. The picture in the catalog was hardly an engineering drawing; it looked like a lithograph out of a nineteenth century copy of *Harper's Weekly*. But it did have dimensions, and the dimensions appeared to fit our boat. I went over it with Chuck. He was dubious, but he couldn't really see why it wouldn't fill the bill.

What a great excuse for a trip! There was time in June after Megan came home from college and before the start of her summer job, so we planned a long weekend's venture to Nova Scotia to visit the Lunenburg Foundry and check out our prospective steering gear. It's an easy trip, because you can take an overnight car ferry from Portland, Maine, to Yarmouth, Nova Scotia. We made our plans, bought our tickets, and on the appointed day drove to Portland and waited in line to drive aboard the *Scotia Prince*.

By all appearances it was a routine ferry line. The blacktop was marked off into staging areas, and these were filled with cars, trucks, and RVs. Motorcycle clubs and antique autos added color. Officials with armbands walked around checking tickets and performing their official functions. Drivers and passengers got out and strolled around the lot to pass the time. Eventually the ship was ready, the steel gangways clanked into place, and we drove aboard. Leaving our camping gear in the mini-van we shouldered our duffel bags, climbed the stairs to the passenger area, and blinked to find ourselves surrounded by tuxedoed waiters offering trays of drinks. The decor, in tasteful pink and purple, looked like the Reno Holiday Inn. Signs pointed to the disco. And everywhere, we saw banks of slot machines. You knew it all along, but we didn't: This was a casino ship. It had never occurred to me that with a few hours in international waters between the U.S. and Canada, what I thought was a ferry was a major recreational opportunity.

For some people. I'm not about to knock the folks who get on the ship in Portland, gamble and drink all night, grab a nap in Yarmouth where the ship turns around, and ride it back to Portland the next day for more of the same. But me, I felt as though I had been penned up for slaughter.

Beth, Megan, and I, country mice in the big city, retired to catch what sleep we could. At dawn we returned to the deck in time to watch the ship working her way through dense fog into the narrow entrance of Yarmouth harbor.

As the ship eased up to her wharf the fog lifted, and we drove off the ramp in sunshine. We were on holiday. We visited Digby and the Annapolis Valley, enjoying the scenery, charm, and friendly people of Nova Scotia. We drove over the mountains, tossed our tent and sleeping bags into a rented canoe, and camped overnight on an island in Kejimkujik National Park. The next day we meandered down the road to the Atlantic coast and the Lunenburg Foundry.

In business since 1891, the Lunenburg Foundry has been supplying the Canadian fishing fleet since the days of wooden schooners. The business has changed slowly with the times, and today they sell high-speed diesel engines for trawlers as well as make-and-break one-lungers for motor dories. We inquired after steering gear and were led through the machine shop and up a set of plank stairs to the upper floor of a vast rickety shipyard building. Rooms of shelves were filled as densely as library stacks with carved wooden patterns of everything the foundry has ever cast. This library has no card catalog; it has men who know every item on the shelves.

"We don't keep that steering gear in stock, not much call for it, but we can cast one up for you." If they've ever made one, then they can make another. The foreman located the patterns on one of the shelves and took the time to show us how its parts fit together just as the finished product would. The machinist agreed to adjust the shaft to fit our steering wheel. Otherwise, the steering gear would be built exactly to the original drawing that bore the date April 7, 1932.

We waited until *Anasazi*'s construction plans were firm before actually ordering the gear, and then it was another eight months before the Lunenburg Foundry finished and shipped it. It arrived carefully packed in a wooden crate, the gleaming brass parts lying in a bed of wood shavings. The whole gear looked like some giant piece of jewelry.

⚓

Together with the architect's drawings, the specifications form the basis for the building contract. They cover everything from the type of epoxy to the design of lifeline stanchions, from engine mounts to paint colors. In that sense they are similar to the specifications for a house, although the specifications for a yacht are more complex than those for a house, for a number of reasons.

First, there is no building code for private, noncommercial boats. It is possible to refer to standards written by organizations such as the American Bureau of Shipping, the American Boat and Yacht Council, Lloyds of London, and the U.S. Coast Guard. Perhaps it is advisable to do so from a legal point of view, but it serves no practical purpose. A small boatbuilder works from experience. He may hold in his head a few of the standards that he's needed in the past, or know where to go to look up sizes of electrical wires, but it is completely unrealistic to expect him to keep going to the books as he plans each day's work, just in case one of the authorities has adopted a standard on this subject. And even if he did go to the books, it takes a sea lawyer to understand them, catch all the exceptions, and know when they apply. In short, it's easy to incorporate volumes of standards into a contract with a few words, but that won't help the builder. The specifications must spell out, clearly and in one place, the materials to be used and how each part of the boat is to be built.

Second, with due respect to the good people who design and build houses, it is more difficult to design and build a successful boat. In addition to providing a comfortable living space with electricity, plumbing, and kitchen appliances, a cruising sailboat must accommodate both a sailing rig and an engine. All this must be packed into about a tenth of the volume of even a small house, and shaped to be driven efficiently through water. The convenience of square, level components is left ashore; boats are made of curves and odd angles. Finally, houses stand still. The boat and everything in it must be strong enough to be picked up and dashed about by ocean waves.

Oh, did I leave something out? Is it a challenge to build a dry basement? Boats are immersed in water full time.

When he first explained to us the process of having a boat built, Bob Ackland suggested that Beth and I write the specifications ourselves. I choose to assume that his suggestion reflects the depth of our experience and wisdom, but it is just possible that our somewhat eccentric opinions figured into his thinking.

Based on a firm foundation of ignorance, I dove into the specifications. Now I was making progress—perhaps too much progress. In our first meeting I had asked Chuck for sample specifications that we could use as a guide. He sent two, and they were helpful, but of course they weren't our boat. The first was the general specification for a 42-foot production boat to be outfitted to the desires of each buyer. The second was a custom-built high-performance 45-footer that obviously would cost three or four times our budget. Both of these specs ran to fifty-odd pages of single-spaced text, and ours would eventually be about the same. (The Appendix shows an outline of our finished specification. The outline alone is six pages long.)

The spec for the production boat was a spare document. Evidently it relied heavily on the fact that the designer knew the builder well and on additional customization and systems to be worked out later for each particular buyer.

The other spec provided more to work from. It had been prepared by the prospective owner of one of Chuck's custom designs, and it obviously was a product of much labor and great care. The 45-foot cruising boat it described was a true gold-plater sporting no end of mechanical systems, from electric windlass to forced-air cabin heat, to a separate diesel engine for use as a pump and generator. Did I think our four anchors were conservative? This boat would carry five. Each system had been carefully planned, thought out, and described in the specification.

So I just needed to lift the topics from the sample spec, eliminate those that didn't apply (remote radio speakers, bicycle hooks), and rewrite the rest to our liking. I started with an overall organization:

1. General (description, materials, standards)
2. Hull and deck construction
3. Machinery
4. Plumbing
5. Electrical
6. Deck
7. Interior
8. Finishes
9. Spars
10. Standing rigging
11. Running rigging
12. Outfitting
13. Owner-supplied items.

Then, with frequent detours for consideration, research, and domestic disputes, I wrote down everything we wanted in each of those areas, using Chuck's spec as a checklist and guide.

Chuck reviewed my draft, took a breath, and tried to be tactful. The problem was, in working from someone else's spec, and without really applying much independent judgment, I had developed an attitude. The spec was too subjective, and it sounded unreasonably demanding. I had adopted phrases like "exceptionally rugged" and "especially reliable." I had read phrases in the model spec such as:

> Turnbuckles should be as big as possible (that is to say, oversize) and of a superior quality that will not be prone to galling.

and

> All necessary [bottled gas] adapters, pigtails, and connectors for use in any country should be provided.

When a builder reads requirements like these he knows that he's in for a lot of research into what products are available, and after the research is through, he still won't know whether what he's found will satisfy the owner. And how is he to quote a firm price for "as big as possible" and "superior quality"?

Perhaps worst of all, that kind of spec gives the builder a picture of the owner as demanding but unspecific, the kind of person who expects the builder to read his mind, even though he has yet to make his mind up. Builders are reluctant to work for such people.

All of this Chuck gently pointed out, and I returned, chastened, to my word processor. As I improved the spec, it became shorter.

⚓

Mornings at our house fell into a routine. Over a first cup of coffee Beth and I would discuss the boat issues of the day: the size of a deck hatch, clearance beneath the bowsprit, placement of the fuel tanks. Then I'd sit at the table and work up the requisite drawing. I'd finish a couple of hours later, and around nine o'clock I'd put boat matters away and get on with the more remunerative tasks of my so-called career.

Completing the drawing usually required some kind of research, perhaps measuring available space from the existing plans, perhaps looking up the strength of 3/8-inch wire rope. So there were trips to the reference books, catalogs, and photocopier.

I was too cheap to provide myself with a proper drafting table. Instead I cut a 2-foot square of chip board, sanded it smooth, and then splurged on a two-dollar plastic rolling ruler. The other toys were a set of ships' curves, engineering templates for drawing circles, an architect's scale rule, lots of pencils, and lots of erasers.

What was I drawing? The details. Chuck's plans laid out the boat's interior, but before the boat could be built someone had to determine the height of each shelf, the angle of each seat back, the thickness of the cushions. Have you ever designed your fantasy house, or den, or kitchen? It was fun to design storage for charts under the double berth, the tip-out trash bin, the portlight for passing lunch to the cockpit.

A typical drawing showed a cross-section through the boat at some point along its length. All of the joinerwork at that point—every cabinet, bookshelf, seat, and tank—was carefully drawn in at scale, with dimensions written in to aid the builder. Finishing one of those drawings took a couple of hours.

Then there was the research. What are the options for attaching and sealing the teak deck planks? Where could we find elliptical bronze portlights? How about horizontal-mount propane tanks? How big are the batteries, and what amperage should we allow for the master switch? What size bronze strapping will be needed to anchor the wires supporting the mast?

The books had some answers, and Chuck and Mark had others. I sent for product specifications and phoned with questions. I learned to appreciate the full meaning of "back to the drawing board."

⚓

Spring became summer, and our schedule kept slipping. We had planned to wrap up the preliminary design by the end of May, but each meeting, each set of revisions to the drawings, was delayed.

I can picture Chuck's dilemma. The *Anasazi* commission had arrived at a slow moment, and Chuck was glad to accept it. Then business picked up. Morris Yachts was enjoying success with its production models of Paine-designed boats. Chuck had drawn a new series of large, high-performance aluminum cruising yachts, with contemporary lines and names chosen from tropical flowers: *Bougainvillea, Frangipani.* Clients began to spring up, both in America and in Europe. An opportunity appeared to collaborate on the design of a 100-foot sailing yacht to be built in Florida. These boats, all far more costly than *Anasazi*, represented Chuck's future. There was customization work, and boat shows, and a monthly design feature for *Yachting* magazine.

Faced with the opportunity to do more and more, Chuck did exactly what the rest of us in the service business do. He overcommitted. At C. W. Paine Yacht Design, Inc., the principal architect, director of marketing, and office receptionist was Mr. C. W. Paine. When you telephoned the office, Chuck answered. When it came time to pay the telephone bill or a draftsman's salary, Chuck pulled a checkbook out of his pocket.

Now, with Chuck piling up frequent flier miles trying to respond to his far-flung clientele, Mark spent his days supervising boats under construction and his nights at the drafting board. Maura Rogers joined the firm, and suddenly the telephone was answered regularly and bills went out on time. Maura kept the photos organized, pulled blueprints, and generally did what she could to free up Chuck and Mark.

With Chuck and Mark juggling the demands of far bigger boats and of builders who represented repeat business, work on *Anasazi* took a back seat. Responses to our questions were delayed for weeks. After each meeting it took a month to schedule the next one.

Meanwhile, Beth and I didn't help speed up the project either. We had no shortage of ideas, thoughts, and opinions. We reviewed each drawing carefully and always ended up with a list of questions, concerns, and changes. I suspect—no, I *know*—that we were providing far more input, and making far more work, than Chuck had expected.

It was early August before we had all the pieces of a preliminary design: the shape of the boat, the basic interior layout, the sail plan, and some construction drawings. It wasn't complete enough to solicit bids, and it contained a few inconsistencies, but it was a coherent picture of *Anasazi*.

Our plan from the beginning was to stop the process at this point for two or three months. Beth and I would use that time to study the design thoroughly and make a list of requested changes. We then would freeze the basic design, and the rest of the design project would consist of adding detail.

It sounds like a good idea, and I think it actually was. By now this project was beginning to look like a felony viola-

The design office: Chuck Paine, Maura Rogers, and Mark Fitzgerald.

tion of the Paperwork Reduction Act. My office had turned into Design Central, with boxes, binders, and stacks of design materials overflowing into the dining room. We had blueprints of each revision, multiple versions of the spec, sketches of installation details, sail plan calculations, engine specifications, reference pamphlets, catalogs, descriptions of other designs for comparison, notes from our last call to Chuck, and notes for our next one. We were living on paper, and it was getting ready to kill us.

Caitlin, our oldest daughter who learned her navigation in the North Atlantic, was by now a college senior. Caitlin has a good eye for design, and we had been keeping her up to date by mailing her copies of the drawings. We sent a few more to her, threw out a few others, and began studying the rest, pouring over every detail, measuring, looking up numbers, paging back and forth among the big blueprint sheets.

Through September we worked on our list of changes, and on the first of October we sent it to Chuck. For example:

1. We've decided to delete the two portlights in the forward end of the cabin, since a large hatch is there. It's no harder to add them later if we need them.

2. The running backstay obstructs passage along the deck. Can we move its anchoring point inboard to the side of the cabin and still swing the dinghy on board?

3. I am very concerned about the strength of the hull in the vertical direction, that is, the pull of the shrouds upward. Seems like we need thicker diagonal veneers, or a vertical veneer, or something. Please refer to enclosed analysis, which suggests to me that we have only half the vertical strength that Nevins Rules would provide. But my engineering is sort of half-baked, so please let me know if I'm not looking at it correctly.

4. Change cross-section shape of bilge stringers so they won't hold water.

5. The keel, particularly its after end, seems thin and potentially weak. I am picturing the boat being driven ashore, which tends to be sideways, and the keel snapping off. I have two concerns:

   a. The attachment of the deadwood to the apron, or keel batten. Perhaps you had this weak spot in mind when you said you had decided to work the hull further down into the keel at station 9.

   b. The construction of the deadwood itself, which is only 4 to 5 inches thick and has all the grain in one direction. Instead of picturing it as a pile of 2 × 6's stacked horizontally, let's put those 2 × 6's in three vertical planes, each oriented 120 degrees from the others. The enclosed drawing tries to convey what I mean.

6. We'd like to move the two angled bulkheads that enclose the head 2 inches to port. Aesthetics. We understand that this will make the head a bit tight.

7. Then we can extend the forward galley counter about 2 inches to port so that its end is in alignment with the starboard side of the mast.

8. For easier cleaning, let's locate the galley post at a corner of the counter, not surrounded by counter top.

9. Is there any reasonable alternative to a plastic muffler?

There were twenty-eight of these detailed issues. Some were nitpicks, some were serious—if occasionally unfounded— concerns, but none of them was a very big change. We hoped to have the modified preliminary drawings back in a couple of weeks so that we could start moving from the world of designing boats into the world of building boats.

⚓

And now the question was upon us: How were we to find someone to build the boat? We had no knowledge of boatbuilders, so of course we asked Chuck's opinion. But it wasn't going to be as simple as taking the architect's recommendation. Chuck has recent experience with a number of builders of fiberglass and aluminum boats, particularly in the market's upper echelons. He knew, though, that the right builder for us would be a small shop that did most of its work in wood. He offered a couple of names, but researching the market would be our job.

I started compiling a list of candidates. Ultimately, we knew we would try to find a shop that could work very efficiently and whose standards made us comfortable. That meant a level of construction and finish that was well above workboat quality, but not to yacht standards of the expense-is-no-object variety.

As yet there was no way to judge those standards. For now we added any shop to our list that was identifiable as a builder of wooden boats and located within reasonable distance. We felt that we needed to be able to visit the builder and return within a day, so the drive from our home to the shop should be no more than three or four hours.

Advertisements in the back of boating magazines offered a number of names. Chuck added a few more, and we had notes on other builders from our early conversation with Bob Ackland. The public library's reference section had a directory of builders of wooden boats. It was six or eight years old, but it provided more names.

It took only a few days to come up with the names of forty builders for the initial list. Chuck reviewed it and marked those that he knew had gone out of business, or that he would suggest we not contact. (I didn't ask him to say why, and he didn't.) He also marked a few with whom he particularly recommended talking. The rest were open questions. The list was down to twenty-six.

I got on the phone and placed calls to all twenty-six. More names dropped off the list: too big a project, don't have time, or just a disconnected telephone. Two or three shops limited their work to traditional plank-on-frame construction. Now we were down to about a dozen candidates, and I started arranging visits to the ones that seemed most likely.

⚓

Paul Rollins's directions led us along pleasant backroads in southern Maine. In late September the hayfields were dry and brown, but the day was sunny and mild. We turned into the driveway, parked by a large gray barn, and ambled inside. The barn was filled with the hull of a traditional schooner nearing completion, 55 feet long, with deck beams of locust, bracing knees of white oak, and frames three inches thick. The hull almost breathed grace and power. This vessel would sail smoothly among the islands in Penobscot Bay or slice through green seas in the North Atlantic. Conning her helm you would feel satisfied that you were out there doing what *should* be done.

Rolled up in my hand were the drawings for *Anasazi*, a family sailboat to be laminated up from sticks you could break over your knee. I felt like a dreamer of very small dreams.

I argued with myself: After the laminating is done my sailboat's hull will be enormously strong, not to mention permanently watertight. Our boat can be worked by one or two people. It will sail to windward, maneuver in harbors, resist rot better than the schooner, and altogether be far more practical for us. At the same time our boat will please the eye as befits her own worthy tradition, and she *is* a wooden boat, too. A fine argument it was, and it almost reassured me.

I remained a bit shaken as we climbed the stairs and Paul Rollins invited us into the apartment he had built for his family in the barn's upper level.

I immediately liked Paul for this apartment. It was full of light, cozy, functional, and enhanced by attractive touches of clever woodwork. We spread the drawings on a low table and talked about building the boat. As we talked, we could see that Paul was living his dream, making a life for himself and his family, building the kinds of boats he wanted to build.

I admired him, but I knew that *Anasazi* was not one of those boats. Paul was committed to traditional construction. He avoided epoxies and polyurethanes because he felt they were dangerous. He would be willing to talk further about building our boat, but we had some fairly fundamental differences of opinion. Although we respected him, it seemed unlikely that we would work well together.

Walter Beckmann and his son Lloyd build boats in Rhode Island. Beth and I found their shop in a converted farm building of white masonry at the edge of an open field a few miles from the western shore of Narragansett Bay.

The Beckmanns have built many kinds of boats, but they specialize in old-fashioned steam launches and family cruising tugboats. If you're looking for a three-chime steam whistle or a good horizontal fire tube boiler, then Walter Beckmann is your man.

These boats are long on charm and a bit short on practicality. So since when is boating practical? Are we so goal driven that we give no respect for charm? Boating is supposed to give pleasure, and who does not understand the pleasure of gliding majestically across the lake in an open launch with gleaming rails, colorful fringed canopy, shining brass boiler, and a wisp of white steam? The term "character boats" has gained a derogatory ring in our world of mass market, most-boat-for-the-money production. But if the alternative is a boat without character (which it generally is), then I'll take a stand for character boats and boat characters.

Walter Beckmann did not strike us as a boat character. He seemed to be a hard-working, hard-headed, experienced builder of boats. He made his living as all boatbuilders do, by matching his customers' demands with the abilities of his shop.

We looked around at the shop's work in progress, and we inspected photos of boats they'd built. We reviewed *Anasazi*'s plans together and discussed construction methods and schedules. Clearly this shop was geared to efficient, no-nonsense construction, if not to the yachting standards that were established in the days of Cornelius Vanderbilt. It was a serious possibility to build *Anasazi*.

One of the builders that Chuck had suggested lived and worked in our own town. We didn't know Damian McLaughlin well, although he and Beth sang together in a community chorus. (Just what Beth was doing singing in The Greater Falmouth Mostly All-Male Men's Chorus is a story for another time.) We telephoned and arranged to meet at Damian's shop.

To reach the shop we navigated a quarter-mile dirt road that winds across a sandy bottom, around a tight turn, and up a rise through a forest of scrub oak. The Toyota bottomed out in the potholes, and stones flew out from under the wheels. The entrance to the driveway was marked by the hull of a sailboat that appeared to have been awaiting restoration for some years now. We pulled in, parked by a lumber pile, and entered the barn-like building.

Along one side of the shop was a long narrow stockroom with a planer standing so that long boards could be run through it. Along the building's other side were benches filled with tools—old-fashioned wooden planes, new-fangled electric grinders, and plenty of everything in between. The open area in the middle had a white planked floor, a high ceiling, and walls lined with more supplies. Overall, the shop would be just barely long enough and wide enough for *Anasazi*.

A door led to a cramped office piled with plans and catalogs. At the back of the shop was a welding rig and an old Bridgeport milling machine, and behind those was a coal-fired forge.

Besides this variety of technologies there were other hints of a multitalented individual who did not take life too seriously. One wall sported a dartboard and posters depicted skiing and board sailing. An airplane wing was in for repair. The wall by the drill press held shelves of twist bits, spade bits, hole saws, and countersinks, and above those someone had written DRILLVILLE.

In his fifties, with gray hair and a bushy gray moustache, Damian moves with energy and thinks quickly. He gave us a summary of his experience: nine trimarans in the 30- to 50-foot range, plus several large catamarans, and a couple of single-hulled sailboats. Much of this work used wood-epoxy construction similar to what we planned for *Anasazi*.

He talked about some of that experience as we looked over *Anasazi*'s drawings. "One thing I've learned is not to start construction until all of the plans are completed. Every time you do it, and you think 'Those little details will be finished in plenty of time', then you don't have some information you need, and it slows you down."

As we delved into the details, Damian seemed enthusiastic about building this boat. "The plans don't call for a stem rabbet, but I think we'd want to build it that way. That's something I can work out with the naval architect." It was a successful meeting: We had found another well-qualified builder, he was interested in the business, and he was located fifteen minutes from our house.

Tom Wostenholme's shop occupied a cavernous Quonset hut just north of Newport, Rhode Island. A cold October rain sent us hurrying across the parking lot to take shelter inside. The shop was inactive and only partially lit, the overcast day increasing the sense of gloom inside. We wandered about in the half dark, looking up at the boats, all of which were old or old-looking. Among the boats were piles of boat parts, and I bumped into a dusty collection of salvaged spars and timbers that might come in handy some day. Everything was cold to the touch.

Tom calls his business Rivendell Marine. One boat bore the name *Gandalf.* We started to notice other references to the hobbit stories of J. R. R. Tolkien. Some were clever; others could charm only a confirmed Tolkien devotee.

The shop was vast and, being a Quonset hut, had a curved roof that soared high above the cradled hulls. Even with the several sizable boats inside there was plenty of excess space. In this dark, cold expanse we waited. We were not optimistic.

Tom arrived, apologized for being late, and led us toward his office. He's a big man with broad shoulders, full beard, and bright blue eyes. His greeting and handshake were warm.

Even better, his office was warm. Although the day outside was dark gray, a large window let in plenty of light. One wall was filled with books about boats and boatbuilding, many that were long familiar to me, others that I'd been wanting to read. My toes started to thaw.

Tom showed us an album of his past boat projects—some new work, some major repairs, all in wood, and almost all of traditional design and methods. We saw that he was particularly pleased with the nice touches, a graceful rail, a carved stem head. We well understood his pride; it seemed like a good idea to work with a builder who found pleasure where we did.

Once again we were confronted by the contradiction in our design for *Anasazi*. We loved the look of traditional boats, but just as much we loved the *thought* of them, the knowledge that a boat is part of a long tradition based on strong timbers and closely fitted joints, a tradition that is passed into each boat by skilled hands on chisel, plane, and caulking mallet. But we also wanted a boat that could be sailed and maintained by a middle-aged couple, spend long periods in the tropics, survive a year or two out of the water, last for many decades without major rebuilding, and, by the way, not leak. Remember the coast of Brazil?

I needn't apologize for my practical desires—we live in an age in which pragmatism requires no apology. I also don't apologize for the impractical desires, because they are aesthetic and cannot be argued. But one boat can only be built one way, and it only reinforces the old cliché that every boat is a compromise. *Our* compromise would be a boat of traditional shape, built of wood, with long keel, bowsprit, varnished rails, and a tall wooden mast. But her construction would be modern, with a laminated skin and plywood decks, held together with gap-filling glue.

Tom's love for traditional wooden boats didn't stop him from being intensely interested in *Anasazi*'s plans. As we talked about her design and future construction, Tom impressed us with his broad knowledge and good sense. Surely the skills from traditional boatbuilding would only improve *Anasazi*. So here we had found a capable builder who shared our aesthetic and who wanted to build a laminated hull. Perhaps this was the perfect combination?

We did have reservations. The hobbit fixation made me uneasy, but, hey, who doesn't have personal idiosyncrasies? The eerie, empty shop left a lingering impression. And I questioned Tom's ability to build *Anasazi* economically. We'd find the answer to that question when he bid on the job.

These weren't the only builders we visited. Experienced, reputable men such as Walter Greene, Tim Hodgdon, Jim

Foley, Kaz Zatek, and Paul Konitzky showed us their work, discussed our plans, and offered their thoughts. We learned from all of them. The list came down to seven builders we thought were good candidates, and who were interested in preparing bids for *Anasazi*.

⚓

While we were visiting builders, Mark was working to update the drawings. There seemed to be no end to the small inconsistencies and details that we needed to deal with, but we hacked away at the list, postponing any corrections that weren't necessary for getting bids. On November 20 the Federal Express driver arrived with the drawings that we would send to potential builders.

I arranged the big architectural drawings and stacks of photocopied specifications into piles on the living room floor, and I crawled about assembling a package for each builder— the folded drawings from Chuck, my joinerwork drawings of the details, the 40-page spec, and a cover letter with instructions. The thick envelopes went to the post office on the day before Thanksgiving. At last we were beyond casual talk and going out into the real world with a commitment to build a boat. We were ready to play for keeps, and we had to ask the question for real: What will it take to build this boat?

Most of the builders had said that they'd need a couple of weeks to prepare their bids, so we asked for responses by December 15. The scheduling allowed me to feel virtuous. As a bidder on government contracts I've often received specifications issued in mid-December, with responses due right after New Year's Day. You can sense the buyer's attitude: We'll let the contractor slave frantically over this thing during the holidays while we relax and wait for the bids to arrive when we come back to work in January. So I tried to reverse the process: Let the bidders finish their work, and Beth and I would use late December to pore over the bid proposals.

My effort, however well intended, was a failure. In my business the deadline for a bid is sacrosanct. A late bid is automatically rejected. Is your bid late by one hour? You might as well drop it directly into the nearest recycling bin; you've done nothing but waste time and trees. Obviously, with those ground rules, deadlines receive the utmost respect.

I soon learned that boatbuilders operate in a different world. We sent our package to a total of seven builders. Two builders decided to bow out. Two builders got the flu. The other three just didn't quite get around to it. By December 15 we had received a few questions but not a single bid.

Over Christmas, over New Year's, and well into January I was telephoning the five remaining contenders. "Yes, sure, I understand. And when do you think you'll be able to finish it?" One by one the bids trickled in.

⚓

We had developed some guesswork about the cost. A magazine article describing one similar boat said that it was built in 6,500 hours. In another article a builder figured that he builds four pounds of boat per hour, so by his reckoning *Anasazi*'s 30,000 pounds would take 7,500 hours. We snapped up numbers like that and multiplied them by possible labor rates. A really hungry builder looking to keep his workers busy might charge as little as sixteen dollars per hour. An established yard with plenty of business might double that number.

For the cost of materials I made some wild guesses and scribbled a column of figures: materials might come to fifty or sixty thousand. And how would overhead be applied? Adding unknowns to unknowns, the possible range of prices began to look enormous.

When the actual bids came in, they were spread as widely as our guesswork had been. Two bids were close to each other at around $350,000. That was simply too high. One bid was under $150,000, based on a labor estimate of 4,100 hours. We didn't believe *Anasazi* could be built that quickly and cheaply, and working with a builder who is losing money most likely would result in extra costs *and* a badly built boat.

The remaining bids, from Damian McLaughlin and Tom Wostenholme, were close to our hopes: labor in the range of 6,500 to 7,000 hours, and a total bid of around $200,000. Some issues still needed to be addressed, but we were elated: Two capable builders had submitted bids within our range. The hardest job would be choosing between them.

⚓

Although we were delighted with the opportunity to make the selection, each of the two bids left us with some discomfort. Damian's bid was so informal as to be hardly a bid at all. He simply worked up a set of numbers on a yellow pad and went over them with us: the number of hours for each worker, shop overhead, materials and other outside costs, and profit.

He was nervous about what he felt was vagueness in the specification. Some of his concerns were understandable. When we specified that "Access to engine, steering gear, chainplate bolts, keel bolts, plumbing fittings, electrical fittings, and all other equipment which may require service shall be provided without requiring destructive disassembly of joinerwork," we raised a red flag in his mind. Although providing access for service is a routine part of competent boatbuilding, if we had been unreasonable in enforcing that specification, we might have been in a continuous state of war.

Some of Damian's concerns, though, were about items that were perfectly clear, or were so minor that they could not possibly have affected his cost. When I specified that the engine controls were to be mounted "near the helm," would knowing precisely *how near* change his bid?

Besides, Damian's cost calculation was frighteningly rough. We knew how rough it was because he had described his costing method to us. He examined the plans and specifications, compared this boat to other boats he'd built, and asked a few old friends about their costs in building similar boats. That was it.

But working at a more detailed level wouldn't have soothed Damian's basic discomfort. At heart, he just didn't want to submit a firm bid. He cheerfully would have given us an estimate and then poured all of his energy and ability into ensuring that the estimate wasn't exceeded, but signing his name to a firm six-figure number felt wrong to Damian.

One of the sources of Damian's anxiety was us. Despite the detailed plans and specifications, I think he wasn't sure that we were realistic, reasonable people to work with. His solution to that uncertainty was to increase communication, which he did in two ways. He marked every place in the spec that seemed vague to him, and he suggested that we agree to confer on each such point as he built the boat. Of course, I was expecting to be closely involved with the construction, so I was happy to agree. He also wanted to show us a sample of his work, not to impress us, but so that we could see his standards and finish work. He wanted to be sure that we had a mutual, realistic expectation of what we'd be getting if he built the boat.

The sample he had in mind was an hour's drive down Cape Cod, and we drove together. On the way we talked about firm price bidding. The exchange was predictable: Damian thought that quoting a price for building a custom boat wasn't possible; I explained that I wasn't able to write blank checks. Now I was the one getting nervous, because it was clear how little confidence Damian had in his estimates.

We arrived at a neat home in Harwich. The front of the house faced the street, and the backyard went down to the water. Damian knocked, and Mrs. Van Buren opened the door. From the moment of her greeting, the warm regard that she held for Damian was obvious. This man had built the boat that she and her husband had enjoyed for ten years. Once or twice they had called him back to make some modification. She trusted him, and when he had an opportunity to further his boatbuilding business, she was pleased to be able to lend her support. This was good.

We walked to the water's edge and began inspecting a large cruising trimaran. Damian pointed out details of construction and finish. "Look, after ten years you can see the seams through the paint." We found a ladder and climbed aboard. The interior was simple, functional, and, as Damian proudly pointed out, lightweight. There was little trim, and nothing gleamed. But the quality of work was good, it had held up well to ten years of weekend sailing, and we saw nothing slipshod. *Anasazi* certainly would be more traditional, more "yachty" in appearance, but the standards of workmanship were solid. We were satisfied with the boat, we were pleased with Damian's concern that we see it, and we were impressed by his obvious excellent relationship with his customer. Also, as we talked casually to people in the community, we began to pick up rumors and stray remarks—everyone spoke highly of Damian McLaughlin.

The drive home was quiet. There wasn't much to say, and as we drove in silence Damian believed he had lost the business. We agreed to arrive at a decision within a week, and to "stay in touch."

Tom Wostenholme also was uncomfortable submitting a firm bid, but he responded in the opposite manner. He worked through the entire project in his head. Meticulously he wrote down a week-by-week schedule for building the boat, what would be accomplished, and how much labor it would take. He also researched the costs of materials, both commodities like lumber and paint, and special items like bronze castings and stainless steel railings. All of this detail and more was set down in 60 pages of worksheets, references, resumes, and promotional material. This is the way I work, with lots of detail and lots of numbers. It made me feel a kinship with Tom.

Despite the thoroughness of his proposal and his excellent references, we did have some reservations about Tom's bid, and I asked to meet with him to discuss his proposal. It only made sense to let Tom put his best foot forward, so I told him our concerns in advance. There were three of them.

First, although Tom had a great deal of experience, he had never built a whole boat of this size. Second, most of his experience was with traditional plank-on-frame boats; he had not built in laminated wood. The third concern was his huge uninsulated shop, which obviously could not be heated. *Anasazi* was to be glued together, and epoxy glue needs temperatures of at least 40 degrees while it cures—warmer is better.

Although Tom's shop was in Newport, almost two hours away, he lived just 15 miles from us, so we arranged to meet at our house. He arrived well prepared.

"You're right that I haven't built a boat this size from the keel up, but all the principles of building a thirty-footer apply to *Anasazi*. When you loft, the lines are longer, but they're the same lines. Then you build molds, only you build more of them. The difference in planking is that your planking is longer. I've been building boats long enough to have confidence that this size difference just isn't a problem.

"And I think there's an advantage in the experience we do have. When you've done as much restoration work as we have, you get to see a lot of what went wrong. Builders who only do new work never really see that. I believe we build better new boats because we know what we have to do so as to avoid the problems we see."

Tom continued through the list. He had not personally built a laminated boat, but he'd worked on several of them and supervised construction on one, and members of his crew had extensive experience in laminated construction. He reviewed the detailed building schedule, showing us why the hull and deck would be completed before winter, and then describing his three heavy-duty shop heaters.

Of course this was a sales pitch—that's what we had asked for—but it made sense. And through it all came a sense of Tom's competence, his commitment to quality work, and his intense desire to build this boat. When he left, I was almost ready to sign up.

It was time to agonize over the decision, and Beth and I agonized. Although the two men were very different, we *liked* each of them. That was important; we were putting our dream in their hands, and for one year we would be working on that dream together. Damian had impressed us with his experience, his facilities for laminated construction, and his excellent reputation. Tom's careful, diligent proposal bespoke a good person to work with, but more important was his love of beautiful details, and our sense that we shared the same values in boats.

In the end, the swing factor was location; Damian's shop was fifteen minutes from home, while Tom's was almost two hours away. We pictured the frequency of our visits and our ability to stay involved in the work.

We decided to accept Damian's bid. With trepidation, I phoned Damian. With regret, I phoned Tom.

3

Together We Build

Engaging the naval architect with a handshake was all well and good, but to build the boat we'd need a contract. All builders have contracts that they've used before; most builders have contracts that they wish they had used before. I didn't take all that too seriously.

Bob Ackland had advised us that there is no "standard" boatbuilding contract and that we should feel free to be creative. My business experience has given me some background with contracts, and I had accumulated some sample contracts from builders in the course of getting bids.

So I had some definite ideas, and I also wanted to keep it simple. The basic provisions covered what was being built, the time schedule, and the progress payments. As Damian and I had agreed, there was a fixed maximum for labor costs and a bonus for coming in under budget. The contract had to deal with insurance, protection of the boat and equipment, change orders, acceptance and warranty, and resolution of disputes. There were a couple of small legalisms about title, liens, and such. That was about it. I wrote a draft.

I felt that the contract should be reviewed by a lawyer, but I wanted to avoid unnecessary expense for both Damian and us. I suggested a procedure that I have used on other occasions, and which I believe makes a great deal of sense. Damian and I would agree on a lawyer. We would meet together with the lawyer, with the understanding that the lawyer is not engaged to represent either of us, but to ensure that we both understand the contract, advise us on possible changes, and help bring us to agreement on any outstanding contractual issues. The point, in addition to saving time and money, is to avoid starting out a cooperative venture with an adversarial process.

There may be lawyers who object to that procedure, which certainly works contrary to the goal of full employment for the legal community. I would hesitate to trust any lawyer who refused that procedure. But, in fact, most of the lawyers I've worked with over the years have been sensible, down-to-earth, and constructive, and Jay Russell has all of those attributes. Damian and I met in Jay's office.

It was fairly clear that for Damian, appearing at a lawyer's office for a contract negotiation was about as pleasant as appearing at a dentist's office for a root canal. He wasn't nervous about building the boat; he was nervous about a contract that he wasn't certain he understood.

Jay talked us through the points in my draft. By convention, this contract was between "Builder" and "Owner." I wanted the Builder to certify, with each invoice, that there were no liens against the vessel. Damian wanted that changed to "to the best of the Builder's knowledge." Fair enough.

We agreed that the Builder would have a 60-day grace period for scheduled milestones, and that the Owner would have a 10-day grace period for payments. We agreed that Damian could regard communication from either Beth or me as binding on the Owner. We agreed on a procedure for naming an arbitrator for any disputes.

The negotiation had gone smoothly and we had it almost wrapped up when Damian turned back to the schedule of milestone payments. "You know, I've never believed that a set of fixed payments is really the best way to build a boat."

I thought Damian had made his peace with this issue, but obviously he had not. I had already agreed to leave the cost of materials as a variable item—we simply would pay the cost of the materials—and I thought this left us exposed enough. Labor was under Damian's complete control; I didn't see any way that I was willing to compromise further. I answered, "The reason we're here today is that you agreed to a fixed maximum dollar amount. These are the milestones that you laid out. If you think they should be different, let's talk about it, but I'm not willing to drop the idea and go to a time and materials contract."

That ended the discussion; we had an agreement. The agreement had a small cloud over it, though. I hoped that Damian would bring the project in under the labor budget, we'd pay a small bonus, and the fact that the labor cost was capped would never be an issue. I was overly optimistic.

⚓

Damian bought 16 sheets of thin plywood and two gallons of white paint. The project was under way.

We arrived at the shop to find the floor covered with white plywood. Nat Bryant, wearing a set of kneepads for the job, was scuttling about on the white floor with pencils, tape measure, and long flexible strips of wood, patiently lofting *Anasazi*'s lines. Lofting—transferring the architect's shapes to full-size curves—is the first step in building a boat.

Chuck Paine had defined *Anasazi*'s shape in the lines drawing of the hull, the slices from the loaf that created sets of contour lines. Since all the lines are wrapped around the same shape, the contour lines from the vertical perspective will cross the lines from the horizontal perspective, much as lines of latitude cross lines of longitude on a globe. The architect, working at a scale of 3/4 inch to the foot on a sheet of Mylar, measures the position of each point where the lines cross. He records these positions in a table of offsets. There are 293 such intersection points in *Anasazi*'s lines drawing, and so the table of offsets for *Anasazi* has 293 entries.

The entry for each point is that point's distance from a baseline, accurate to the nearest sixteenth of an inch. Discerning a sixteenth of an inch drawn at 3/4-inch scale means judging each measurement on the drawing to about four thousandths of an inch. It is a painstaking job that requires good light and a habit of accuracy, and Mark Fitzgerald had done it well. By convention, he recorded each measurement in feet, inches, and eighths of an inch, with a plus sign indicating the odd sixteenth. A distance of 4 feet, 7 and 5/16 inches is written 4-7-2+. The metric system has not penetrated far into American boatbuilding.

Now Nat Bryant was using Mark's table of offsets to place each point at full scale on the white lofting floor. Nat used red, green, and black pencils to join the points in smoothly curved lines, regenerating at full scale the lines originally created by the architect—the sections, waterlines, and buttocks that define the shape of the hull. This process required several days.

Nat was Damian's first choice to lead the boatbuilding crew. Later Nat would assign tasks to others, but with the whole project dependent on the accuracy of the lofting, Nat was now working alone.

In his early thirties, Nat isn't especially tall, but his thin frame gives him a rangy appearance. His small scraggly beard seems to adorn his chin by default rather than by design. Except on the hottest summer days, it seemed to me that he wore the same faded red fleece pullover and torn jeans from the first day of lofting to the day the boat left the shop.

If Nat gives a visual impression of sloppiness, that impression is immediately dispelled by his work. As a craftsman he is both skilled and orderly.

Also, he must be one of the most intelligent people I've ever worked with. Absorbed in some problem of mounting the steering gear, he can jump without a pause to a question about the support for the bowsprit, immediately recalling the dimensions of each piece and minor decisions that were made weeks before. He can toss off a sentence like "The deck camber increases the coaming height as it angles outboard and forward" more fluently than I can order lunch.

Damian McLaughlin and Nat Bryant.

On that first day, Nat got up from his work, smiled, and we all introduced ourselves. In the months to come the scene would be repeated many times: Nat busy on the work in progress when Beth and I would arrive, always with some matter to discuss. At best, our mission would add some complication to his day, some additional detail to be thought out: How are we going to enclose the autopilot drive and still have adequate clearance behind the steering wheel? Just what size shall I cut the galley sink unit? At worst, we would bring bad news—a part unavailable, a problem found in some part of the work.

No matter how good the relationship, the arrival of the Owner wanting time and attention will not improve the Builder's day. Nevertheless, Nat never failed to greet us with a smile and make us feel welcome. There were times when I know that it must have been an effort; it was an effort that I appreciated.

⚓

Whenever a boat is afloat it is in constant motion. Even in the quietest anchorage a gentle breeze will incline the hull slightly to one side, then to the other. Motion of people on board will change her trim. Even the changing level of water in the tanks or the shifting of food and supplies moves the boat slightly and changes its attitude in the water.

The concepts of level and plumb, convenient artifices ashore, lose their usefulness on a boat afloat. Knowing that, I was surprised to learn how important they are in building that boat.

Damian and Nat stretched a level wire just below the rafters of the shop. The wire ran the length of the shop, down its center. Dropping plumb lines from the wire, they carefully projected the centerline onto the floor. Every part of the boat would be set up and positioned with reference to that centerline. The hull would be built with its waterline level. Bulkheads, the boat's interior walls, would be built plumb, coplanar with the radius of the earth. Carpenters' levels, useless on a floating ship, would be employed continually during its construction.

If building a boat by laminating is different from building plank-on-frame, the difference is not apparent at the start of construction. The lofting process is essentially the same for the two methods. And the next step for either method is to set up the shape of the boat with backbone and cross-sections. Perhaps the largest difference at this stage is that laminated hulls generally are built upside down.

Mike McGowan arrived on the job. Having limited experience building boats, but wanting more, Mike had signed on as an apprentice-level worker. The wage was low, and he could be assured of being assigned the routine, less-skilled tasks, but he would be building a wooden boat with some of the best.

Mike was in his twenties, solidly built with dark curly hair. He was good-humored and enthusiastic from the first time I saw him to the last, in spite of spending some full days on tasks that would have bored me to a sullen dullness in the first half-hour.

Mike was sorry he'd missed the lofting, but happy to be here now. "I want to start right at the beginning. I want to see all the parts." When Mike needed to cross the room, he didn't walk, he ran. Sanding cured epoxy and sweeping out the shop were still far in Mike's future.

With *Anasazi*'s sections lofted on the white floor, Mike set to work building molds. Each mold is a cross-section of the hull. Since the hull is upside down, the mold has the shape of an arch. The molds serve as frames to determine the form of the hull, but they are temporary. After the hull is built over them they are removed and discarded.

Mike transferred the outline of each section from the loft floor to a sheet of Mylar. Mylar is a flexible transparent plastic that, unlike paper, does not stretch. From the Mylar pattern for each section Mike built a plywood mold.

The molds were to be spaced twenty inches apart along the length of the hull, except in those few places where a permanent bulkhead could serve instead. As each mold was completed, Mike stacked it against the wall, and as the days passed the stack of these graceful arches grew thicker. Each one was notched where the structural timbers would cross it, and the lengths of the upright legs placed the waterline of each mold at the same distance below the taut wire over head.

As Mike worked on the molds, Hugh Popenoe built *Anasazi*'s transom, the broad surface that forms the stern. Hugh (his last name is pronounced "poppa-no") is pushing thirty. With his round glasses he looks only a tweed sport coat away from an assistant professorship, but such an inference would be dead wrong. When Hugh isn't building boats for a living, he's building them for fun. After a week of working on *Anasazi*, we'd often find Hugh back in the shop on Saturday assembling his light rowing dory. You'd think that boats are his first love, but alas, Hugh's first love is wind surfing. Cape Cod provides some spectacular oppor-tunities for the sport, and Hugh is a spectacular wind surfer. Somewhere lower on Hugh's list of enthusiasms, but still well above any academic endeavors, is the brewing of a rich brown beer which he supplied to the after-work gather-ings. Hugh can give the impression of living life on the edge—sometimes on the edge of another planet—but when it came to building *Anasazi* Hugh was a solid member of the team, able, willing, and cheerful.

Anasazi's transom is a curved flat surface, like a playing card flexed between your thumb and fingers. The curve is a gentle arc, with a radius of 11 feet. Like the rest of *Anasazi*, the transom is hell for stout. Over a curved form 7 feet wide, Hugh built up layers of wood: 1/4-inch Douglas fir in three alternating diagonal layers, a vertical layer of 3/4-inch Douglas fir, and a horizontal layer of 1/4-inch mahogany. That's just under 2 inches of laminated wood. Bulletproof.

Meanwhile, Nat was building up *Anasazi*'s stem, the timber that forms the forward end of the boat's central spine, defining the profile of the bow. With dividers and bevel square he took widths and angles from the lines on the loft floor and reproduced them in three dimensions in Douglas fir.

So with March slipping away the shop buzzed with activity as the team built parts for later assembly: Hugh at the stern, Mike in the middle, Nat at the bow. Routines became established. The shop radio stabilized at WMVY—album rock. Work began at 8:00 and ended at 5:30. The long work day permitted the crew to take every other Friday off. Those weekend extenders came to be known as Good Friday. Working Fridays were observed with an "executive lunch" at what may be the greasiest diner on the upper Cape.

⚓

By the first weekend in April we had a problem. Chuck Paine had promised completed construction drawings by March 18, and they were nowhere in sight. Chuck had sent the final lines drawing and table of offsets barely in time for lofting to begin. Now the lofting was completed, and construction of the large parts that controlled the shape of the hull were well under way. The lines drawing is only a contour map, though; the builders desperately needed the structural drawings that we still didn't have. Damian gave the crew a week off, and I faxed a note to Chuck:

To: Chuck Paine
From: Gary Schwarzman
Date: April 5, 1992
Re: Schedule

To come right to the point, work on the boat has stopped, the design work is badly behind schedule, and we are losing confidence in your ability to support construction with timely drawings.

At this point we need to agree on a schedule for production of the following items. This schedule needs to allow not only for completion of the drawings in time for construction, but sufficiently in advance to allow for turnaround of problems discovered and to give Damian a reasonable amount of time for advance planning.

1. Complete construction drawings for the hull, deck, and house. The most immediate requirements, the lack of which is stopping work, are listed on the attached page. But the complete construction drawings are overdue.

2. Rudder construction and attachments; gudgeons, bearings, prop aperture.

3. Construction detail of mooring bitts, mast partners, knees, support for running backstays.

4. Ballast casting drawing.

5. Tanks.

6. Weight study, centers, etc.

7. Spars; specifications for rigging.

8. Finished deck plan.

9. Engine installation drawings.

We need the first item (construction drawings) this week. Since they were promised March 18, I don't think that's an unreasonable expectation.

I recognize that you have competing business commitments and priorities, but over the past two months *Anasazi* has not received nearly as much work as was required or promised, and there's now a substantial deficit to be made up.

If we are to continue working together, we need to have a mutually agreeable schedule for the above work, together with your serious commitment to meet that schedule.

Beth and I will telephone on Monday.

⚓

I was feeling abused, and I was embarrassed at failing to hold up my end of the project with Damian. So I tried to talk tough. Was it only talk? In fact, what could I do but plead? The boat was begun, we were committed to the design, and yet the project needed a good deal of additional work by a proficient naval architect. Were we completely at the mercy of Chuck's goodwill and sense of fairness? Well, yes and no.

I wanted Chuck to finish the job. I wanted *Anasazi* to be started and finished as a Chuck Paine design, with designer, builder, and owner taking satisfaction from a well-executed project and a splendid boat. By far the best outcome would be for Chuck to pick up the pace, make up for lost time, and get the project back on track. That was Plan A.

But suppose Plan A didn't work? Suppose that C. W. Paine Yacht Design, Inc., ceased to exist next week. Was there a Plan B? Would we still build *Anasazi*?

You bet we would. I had no illusions about my qualifications in naval architecture, but by now at least I wasn't a complete ignoramus. And, hey, the hull shape and sail plan were done! I would need to find another qualified designer, perhaps a recent naval architecture graduate who was hungry for the work. He would provide the engineering and the drawing skills; I would provide the knowledge of this boat. Between us, we could get the job done. That was Plan B.

Plan B—rolling up our sleeves and taking over the design—did sound like fun, but I knew it was a poor second choice. It would mean stopping the project for weeks or months. That would be unfair to the crew and probably costly. It also would delay *Anasazi*'s launch. It would mean destroying relations with Chuck, which I didn't want, and I had no idea what intellectual property issues there might be in the partial design. Finally, it would consume even more of my time. I would be forced to abandon all pretense of continuing to meet my business responsibilities, which did, after all, have a distinct financial relationship to this project.

No, Plan B was not attractive, but it did exist.

On Monday morning Beth and I telephoned Chuck. As I dialed, I was nervous. I would not have wanted to place a bet on the outcome of that call.

"I got your note, and all I can say is 'You're right.' We've been awfully busy here, but that's no excuse, and we want to do what needs to be done for your boat."

I began to breathe again. We went through the list of what drawings were needed. Chuck promised to send enough design material to let work resume within a few days, and to follow up with a schedule for the rest of the design work. I reported back to Damian with great relief.

Sure enough, the following afternoon the fax machine did its sound and light show of beeps and flashes, and out spewed Chuck's schedule for the remaining drawings: construction plan, rudder detail, engine installation, tanks, deck plan, spars and rigging, all laid out on a schedule beginning mid-April and ending on May 20.

Nat, Hugh, and Mike returned to work the following Monday, and every day they transformed more wood from lumber into a boat.

⚓

Another problem surfaced in mid-April. In the drawing of *Anasazi*'s stern on the loft floor, Nat and Damian couldn't make the edge of the transom meet the hull in a fair curve.

In addition to being curved, the transom slopes at about a 45-degree angle to the vertical. Lofting a curved raked transom into the curved lines of a hull is a problem in conceptual geometry, which is more than my poor brain can handle. That is why I will never know to my own satisfaction whether there truly was a flaw in the design or whether Nat and Damian just didn't quite get it right. These things I do know:

1. I care about the shape of the transom, because I believe that the transom, more than most parts of a sailboat, can be strikingly beautiful or strikingly ugly.

2. The lines drawings show three perspectives, one horizontal and two vertical. Because this transom is at a 45-degree angle, its shape isn't clearly shown on the lines drawing.

3. Because of items 1 and 2, early in the design process I asked Chuck to sketch the transom as it would appear. That sketch remained part of the design drawing, but on careful inspection it was not consistent with the lines and offsets.

4. When the impasse arose, Chuck Paine drove from Camden, Maine, to Damian's shop. As Nat, Damian, and I stood and watched, Chuck worked on his hands and knees on the white painted floor with pencil, squares, and battens and efficiently lofted the transom. It was an impressive demonstration of a complex skill.

5. Weeks later, after the transom was built and set in place, it was apparent that, although the hull lines faired to the transom, the result was ugly. Instead of the graceful oval that characterizes the Alden designs, this transom sagged at the edges. It appeared to have jowls, or something worse. Nat spent a couple of days with a saw, fairing battens, and, thanks to his fine eye for graceful lines, improved the shape.

The transoms of the better Alden schooners and the fishing vessels from which they grew seem to be the natural termination of the gentle curve of the hull, accenting that curve and adding a smooth oval that contributes its own beauty. *Anasazi*'s transom does just manage to avoid ugliness, but it is far from the handsome shape that I had envisioned.

⚓

Damian calls it the magic moment in boat building, and Beth and I couldn't agree more. After weeks of drawing and sawing, the molds are set upright every 20 inches like dominoes, with the transom at the stern and the stem at the bow. Your eye easily follows the curve made by their edges, and your imagination jumps the voids between to create a smooth surface. It is the first time you can see the shape of the boat.

We admired the bow. We admired the stern. We admired the port side and the starboard side. Then we realized that the boat was upside down, and we changed our minds as to which *was* the starboard side.

Yup, it's a good shape.

We walked through the side of the hull, which was easy enough because the hull didn't exist yet. The principal bulkheads were in place, and we could see the interior spaces: the galley, the saloon, the forward cabin.

Damian asked, "Well, are you surprised to see how the spaces actually look?"

We had spent more than a year carefully visualizing each of those spaces. On the drawings we had moved a counter an inch here, a bulkhead two inches there. We had measured the space required to pass by a table, to put your feet up on a settee, to brace your hips in the galley, to pull up your pants in the head.

Now the visions in our minds and the drawings on paper were before us in wood. Although we had neither drawn the lines nor fitted the wood, we had felt immersed in both processes.

We were not surprised.

⚓

*The magic moment. With the molds in place
you can see the shape of the boat.*

While Nat continued to shape the keel members, Mike spent several days running long Douglas fir planks through a table saw to produce hundreds of strips as thick as your finger. The crew fitted these strips into place on the mold structure and glued them to one another along their edges. The inner layer of the hull took shape.

As the strips were glued and fastened on, excess glue squeezed out from between them and dripped down the inside of the hull. The dripping glue had to be wiped up before it hardened, and this job fell to Mike. Patiently, he worked in the semidark beneath the hull, scraping off the dripping epoxy. When he returned for a second day of this messy task, Mike came prepared with a shower cap. He took some ribbing, and he did look a bit silly, but having experienced a bit of epoxy in my own hair, I wish I'd been clever enough to wear a shower cap.

Soon the molds were completely covered with strips of Douglas fir. The epoxy hardened, and hours of power grinding with course sandpaper removed the excess glue and smoothed the seams. It wasn't a boat yet, but it was a boat-shaped object that would float.

Laying thin strips of wood across a framework, it's all too easy to create dents and ripples. The crew had been careful, but it was still necessary to squint along every part of the surface to find the high and low spots. Even better, Nat ran his hands over every square foot. Where his touch revealed any violation of the hull's fair curves, his red marking pen circled the patch for correction. Only after the first layer of planking was faired to Nat's satisfaction did the crew start building up the layers of wood.

The Douglas fir veneer had been stacked and waiting since it arrived from the mill, long and wide like painters' planks, but thin as a window pane. The crew placed each piece diagonally on the hull, sawed it to fit, numbered it, and removed it to another stack. Later they would glue it all into place, and they were getting ready to work fast and cover as large a piece of the hull as possible during the working time of the epoxy glue.

One morning Damian brought in a couple of additional helpers, everyone took his station, and the clock started. Two men spread glue on the hull. Two others chose numbered lengths of veneer from the stacks, brushed glue on them, and passed them up to two more workers who lightly stapled them into place. Damian stapled, mixed glue, and kept an eye on the ordered frenzy. Square yards of hull were covered quickly.

As time ran out, Damian taped a perforated vacuum hose on the work and then spread a sheet of heavy plastic over it. Everyone joined in to tape down the edges of the plastic for an air-tight seal, and Damian started up the big vacuum pump. As the pump sucked out the air, the plastic began to press against the glued veneer. The crew listened for the hisses that indicated air leaks and jumped to apply more window putty and tape. Now the pressure gauge rose as the pump pulled a good vacuum.

We live under the pressure of the atmosphere all the time, but we seldom put it to such clever use. Now ten pounds of

The inner layer of planking is Douglas fir strips, edge-glued and fastened temporarily to the molds. Battens help to keep the strips fair.

pressure on each square inch was holding the lamination onto the hull while the epoxy set.

⚓

We had made a substantial payment to Damian at the start of the project, and the next payment was due on completion of the hull. But before that completion occurred, Damian phoned. "I'd like to talk with you about the cash flow on this project. The first payment is just about gone, and I'll need to come up with some additional cash so the guys can keep getting paid. I'd go to the bank with this, but I've just changed banks, and it's going to take some time to get that situation in order. So the best solution would be if you could see your way clear for some kind of advance on the next milestone payment."

Diagonal layers of Douglas fir veneer
crisscross the hull. While the glue was curing,
the veneer was held in place by the suction
of a vacuum pump.

To be truthful, I had been expecting Damian to run low on cash, because I knew that he'd underestimated the cost of materials by maybe $15,000. Back when we were evaluating the bids I had mentally added that $15,000 to Damian's bid, because I was pretty sure I'd be paying it. Ultimately, the actual cost of materials was my responsibility, but the payment schedule was based on Damian's low estimate, so his running out of cash was predictable.

But not quite so early in the project. Although I had never seen an overall labor projection—I'm sure that none ever existed—I sensed that progress had fallen a bit behind the financial curve. It made me nervous, but I agreed to a partial payment against the future completion of the hull.

⚓

Layer upon layer of wood, then a thin sheathing of fiber-glass cloth on the outer surface, some filling and fairing, and the hull was finished. It so nearly filled the shop that it was impossible to stand back far enough to see the entire hull at one time. Two people walking around the hull would have had to walk single file.

As the hull was taking shape, Damian realized that the boat might fit in his shop, but there would be no room left for the building crew. Quickly, he constructed an annex—a whole new building shed—connected to the shop. Railroad ties served as the foundation; lumber and corrugated plastic formed the walls and roof. A floor was an unnecessary luxury; graded gravel would do. With jacks and rollers the crew moved the hull out the front of the shop and into the new, larger space. The two spaces were connected, so the stationary tools, gluing tables, and supplies in the shop were handy to the boat in progress.

One Sunday afternoon, with the hull recently moved into its new home, we paid a visit. The shop was deserted, and the upside-down hull stood alone in the quiet. Its resin coating was white, and the hull's fair, smooth surface seemed to glow in the dim light. We climbed up the scaffolding and out onto the upturned bottom of the hull. Then Megan and I couldn't resist it: we dropped to our seats and slid down the slick curved surface, landing on our feet on the gravel floor.

⚓

Damian set a Thursday in August as the day to turn the hull right side up. We asked for permission to bring the makings for a party to follow the event, and Damian agreed. (Damian and I share the habit of answering "yes" to any question with the word "beer" in it, just to be on the safe side.)

Although Damian couldn't actually refuse to let us watch, it was clear that he wasn't entirely happy to let the operation become a spectator sport. Maybe it was just a nervous slip of the tongue when he told us that they would turn the

*A layer of fiberglass holds a thick epoxy
coating. Now is that the port side or the
starboard side?*

hull on Thursday afternoon—after he'd just told his crew
he hoped they'd finish the job before lunch. This was too
dramatic a moment to be missed, so I showed up at 8:30 A.M.
to see the preparation. By midmorning I telephoned Beth:
the job was starting in earnest. In no time Beth arrived
with the Toyota mini-van loaded down with the chicken,
potato salad, and chocolate cake that we'd made the night
before, plenty of beer and ice, Megan, Megan's friend, Fleur,
who was visiting from France, a camera, and several rolls
of film.

We stayed out of the way, and the crew did a good job of
appearing to ignore Megan and Fleur as they climbed around
snapping photos.

How do you turn over a 5,000-pound object that is 42
feet long inside a building that is just the size of the object
itself? Easy. First you lift it, then you spin it, then you set it
down. Rope lifting slings were rigged under the hull and
run through pulleys hanging from the rafters. The idea was

to raise the boat by tightening up on the slings. Then, with the slings running through the pulleys, you roll the hull over in place. Once the boat has rolled over, you slack off on the slings and set it down. Piece of cake.

Bracing poles supported the rafters. Pulleys and ropes dangled in the right places. Cable winches were installed in the slings to allow them to be taken up. First one end, then the other, an inch at a time, Damian took up slack, and the hull began to rise. Now it was clear of the ground. From time to time something settled under the weight and a component needed readjustment. Now the hull's a few inches off the ground. Now, real easy, start to turn her over. A little more, a little more, and then a loud crack. With an explosive sound, something gave way, and the hull dropped.

In fact, I did not go into shock. I had anticipated that something might go wrong, and it seemed only fair that if we were going to intrude on the effort, we had to be prepared to take surprises with equanimity. For a few seconds no one knew just what to do. Hugh had been perched high, bracing himself against the hull, but he had jumped clear. It was quickly determined that no one was hurt. Nat had the right instinct: "First we've got to stabilize the hull right where it is. Then we can work on solving the problem." Damian concurred.

With blocks and fenders the crew braced the hull so that it couldn't roll or fall further. Hugh scrambled into the rafters to inspect the structure. The bracing that was intended to hold the pulleys apart from each other had given way. That bracing was reinforced and moved back into position, and the whole arrangement reinspected. The lines were tightened, and the process started again.

In another hour the hull was being eased into position, right side up.

Although I didn't realize it at the time, Damian inspected the hull carefully and found no damage at all except for superficial scratches. The fact that the floor was gravel helped, but the whole event only bolstered everyone's confidence: This was one strong boat.

By now it was late afternoon, and the only thing left was to go to the veranda for barbecued chicken, beer, and wise-

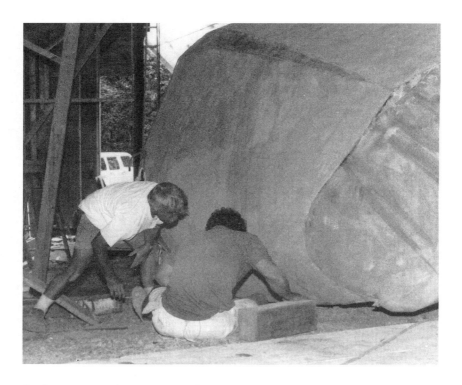

Partway over, a tense moment.

cracks about dropping boats. Friends and sweethearts showed up, and the participation of our two college-age young women didn't hurt the boat builders' morale. And out in the dark shop, *Anasazi* was upright on her keelson.

⚓

Beth and I knew from the outset that if we were going to afford this boat, then we were going to work constantly and vigorously to hold the cost down. Cost was an important issue when we chose strip plank construction, when we wrote the specifications, and when we selected Damian to build her. But we were going to be more active than that: we were going to scrounge materials and parts, and we were going to provide labor.

*Now she's going over smoothly. Only the
plywood bulkheads stiffen the hull, but it's
immensely strong. Hugh watches as the hull
rolls upright.*

Usually we managed to avoid taking our cost-consciousness
to extremes. It made no sense for us to try to buy lumber
and glue; Damian knew his needs, and he knew the suppliers. Even though there was no contractual incentive to keep
the cost of materials down, we completely trusted Damian
to buy as inexpensively as reasonably possible. No problem
there; that's Damian's style. He took pride in reporting, "I
was talking with a shop over in Mashpee that has a two-
inch stainless steel prop shaft that was bent. They can't get
it absolutely straight, so they can't use it again, but it's
only off by a few thousandths, and it'll be fine for your rudder post." Of course the imperceptible bend that would con-
demn a spinning propeller shaft would make no difference
whatsoever to a slowly turning rudder.

We also felt that we shouldn't be working in Damian's
shop. Some builders have permitted this, and Damian offered the possibility when we first talked, but it didn't make

sense to me. Suppose I worked too slowly, or I messed up and created extra work? Suppose I did a job poorly; how could I demand more of the builder? This was my boat, so how could I avoid constantly monitoring everyone else's work? Every worker needs some privacy from the boss and from the customer. We'd visit the shop frequently, but we shouldn't live there.

So we wouldn't work in Damian's shop, and we wouldn't get in the middle of routine purchases of materials. There were many other items, though, where Beth and I could save money by tracking down the parts we wanted, then making our own decisions when it came to cost trade-offs. Besides, scrounging is an old tradition in our family. When we were remodeling our Cape Cod house, the kids would come home after school each day and check on our progress. One day I reported, "Well, after we got that kitchen wall torn out, we made a trip to the dump." The ten-year-old knew what to expect. "Oh," she said, "Did you find anything good?"

On both coasts of the United States, in low rent locations but not far from the waterfront, marine consignment shops struggle along selling one person's old boat equipment to another. Although these businesses operate with a reasonable markup and no inventory cost, somehow they rarely survive for long. They pop up like the spring flowers, live for a year or two, then wilt and disappear. We haunted these places.

One such shop clung to the side of San Bruno Mountain overlooking San Francisco Bay. Beth had joined me on one of my business trips to California, and we dropped in on a Saturday. We found the usual assortment of fittings, including a brass hand pump that now supplies our galley sink. But the great find was a heavy brass pedestal, about waist high, with a spoked brass steering wheel attached. This had possibilities. I didn't want a wheel on a pedestal, but we could mount the wheel on its own steering shaft, and use the strong, attractive brass pedestal for mounting the steering compass.

How much did they want for it? Eight hundred dollars. Considering that the modern equivalent, new, costs about twice that, it wasn't all that bad a deal. But still it was a lot to pay, especially for something whose principal use these days is to decorate the lobby of a fern bar. So I offered half their price, and the offer was accepted immediately. That response always raises visions of the clever seller smirking up his sleeve at the fool who would actually pay *four hundred dollars* . . . But the deal was done. The pedestal came apart into two pieces that weighed down our suitcases, and the steering wheel went home as carry-on baggage.

Eventually, with the investment of time, solder, and elbow grease, our purchase was transformed into a matching wheel and binnacle that lends *Anasazi* a handsome touch.

Back home, another salvaged item came from a warehouse sale. Signs posted around town advertised a Saturday sale of discards and clearance items at the local ministorage lot. Beth and I showed up and waded past piles of broken filing cabinets and used motel furniture. One garage was filled with old sinks. Wait—look again. These were deep stainless steel sinks, of heavy duty construction, including stainless drain boards. The man said they came from a lab at Harvard Medical School. That line may be true and it may not, but it sounded good. The sink unit, cleaned up and trimmed to fit, soon was ready to install on *Anasazi*.

Over the years of maintaining old boats my legendary thrift has led to some productive, if somewhat irregular, sources of supply. One of these is Alco Metals, a scrap yard in San Leandro, California. Besides the usual piles of rusty pipe and I-beams, Alco has well-sorted shelves of brass, copper, and stainless steel. On another business trip I made a small detour into San Leandro's industrial quarter to visit Alco.

Dressed in business clothes—white shirt, wool trousers, jacket, and tie—I felt constrained, awkward, and conspicuous as I pawed through piles of brass cut-offs and climbed up the racks that held stainless steel pipe. With notebook and tape measure I puzzled out ways to meet *Anasazi's* needs from the scrap metal available. As I worked out modified plans for mast and boom fittings, railings, compass housing, and a dozen other items, my pile of metal tubes, sheets, and bars grew on the warehouse floor. When I was finished the pile weighed 240 pounds. Even after the cost of shipping it, that pile of scrap metal saved the project about a thousand dollars.

Another material we'd need was teak. Most of the wood in *Anasazi* is Douglas fir and Honduran mahogany, which are readily available and inexpensive as quality boat lumber goes. Damian bought that. But there were some specific uses for which teak's strength and weather resistance made it the best choice: handrails along the top of the cabin, brass and teak gallows to support the boom, a platform for the bowsprit. It only came to about seventy-five board feet, too small an order for the wholesaler. The local retail supplier wanted eight hundred dollars for the teak. I used a family visit to New Jersey as an opportunity to improve on that.

Deep in southern New Jersey is the town of Mays Landing, where the pine barrens meet the tidal estuaries of the coast. If you extend the Mason Dixon line due east, it runs north of Mays Landing. There, with long sheds extending from the oiled road back into the pine woods, Guardsmen Woodwork is a business that tries to remember the days when wooden products were essential to America's economy, when wooden parts were needed for industrial machinery, farming, and fishing gear.

Those days are becoming harder to remember. Today Steve Pinkos, who runs Guardsmen, needs to stay flexible to keep the business going. He makes some specialty products where he can undersell the competition: wooden spools for rope and cable, swim platforms for sport fishermen. He also sells hardwoods.

In plaid shirt and full beard, Steve led me through his sheds, past heavy cast iron machinery, to shelves that showed the cut ends of thousands of board feet of teak lumber. I selected the pieces that met *Anasazi*'s needs. Steve had a workman surface the boards. I stacked them on the roof of the Toyota van and tied them down. It was an inter-esting morning, and it saved *Anasazi* three hundred dol-lars.

Away from the main port of Jakarta, Indonesia, is the old port of Kalibaru. Here the rotting wharves are crowded with the *pinisi*, traditional lumber schooners, perhaps 60 to 90 feet long. They are primitive and they are rough, but they are also graceful, with raked masts, long bowsprits, and steering oars angled off their sterns.

The year was 1986, long before we began work on *Anasazi*, and I was there. I don't travel overseas regularly, but an odd set of happenstances had taken me to Jakarta on busi-ness. In fact, I wasn't terribly busy, and there was ample time for some sightseeing. For me, of course, that meant hanging around the waterfront.

Not far from the docks were some of the typical market stalls that form the general stores of Third World cities, selling housewares, hardware, and the like. Tucked among them was one stall that stopped me cold. It was stocked with old navigation instruments—compasses, sextants, a pelorus or two. A couple of dozen of these instruments filled shelves surrounding the high stool on which the small, thin dealer perched. Were they salvaged? Certainly. Stolen? Who knows?

Perhaps foolishly I spent no time on the sextants, be-cause I had no confidence that I could determine whether they were damaged. After all, if a sextant has been dropped its frame could be slightly bent and the instrument ren-dered useless. I didn't know enough about them to buy an unknown used sextant.

A compass, though, is a simple thing. If it appears to work, then it works. A 6-inch brass compass caught my eye. The manufacturer had inscribed its name in the gleam-ing bezel: W. Ludolph, of Bremerhaven and Hamburg. Its circular card was divided into the old-fashioned points— north, north-by-east, north-northeast, and so forth—as well as the modern 360-degree circle. Brass mounting gimbals would keep the compass level while the ship pitched and rolled.

I held the heavy brass bowl in my hands, rotated it sideways, tipped it back and forth. The compass worked smoothly. The vendor must have thought I was crazy to pay fifty dollars for it. It went home in my suitcase.

At that time there was no thought yet of *Anasazi*, and the compass resided in our living room, decorating the end of a bookshelf. But I knew that some day in the future there would be another boat. This was just one little step in preparation for that day.

The wood of the locust tree is as close to the perfect material for boats as God has made. It is moderately hard, very strong, and can be worked well with tools. It holds screws firmly and accepts glue reliably. Given a clear finish, locust is beautiful. It is so resistant to rot that everywhere it grows, poles cut from the locust have been driven into the ground to serve as long-lived fence posts.

Naturally, lumber yards don't sell this superb wood. To get locust, you must locate a supply at a specialty dealer or else find your own stand of trees. We did the latter with some help from Hurricane Bob, which careened across Cape Cod in the summer of 1991. Shoreline roads were washed out by the sea, electricity was out for weeks, boats were driven onto the rocks, and a large shade tree landed on our house.

All over town, heavy branches and whole trees were strewn about. Some of these trees were locust trees. My discretion and judgment were no match for the powerful lure of free boat lumber.

Having no proper equipment whatsoever, I charged ahead on a dumb and excessively laborious undertaking. With a bow saw I cut logs in the woods. With a rope to the trailer hitch on the much-abused Toyota mini-van I dragged them out. I squared up the logs with a tiny electric chain saw whose best use is trimming shrubbery. I set the timbers outside to dry and lost most of them to checking and splitting.

But locust is tough, and a few timbers survived in spite of my misguided efforts. I showed them to Damian. Damian is universally admired for his "can do" attitude. Occasionally that admirable quality exceeds his good sense. "Sure, I guess we can use those if they're dry enough. You better paint the ends and set them where they'll get a good breeze. And keep the rain off them."

Just as I had spent far too much time and effort procuring those free timbers, Damian's crew used valuable hours in truing, planing, and shaping them. But the most powerful hurricane to hit Cape Cod in thirty years has supplied *Anasazi* with a pair of stout mooring posts. Their heels are notched and bolted into the stem timber, and heavy deck beams reinforce them in every horizontal direction. In turn, the mooring posts anchor the bowsprit and, indirectly, help to support the mast.

During World War II, Rhode Island's Quonset Point was its own small military city. (You'd been dying to know where Quonset huts come from, right?) Today it's a quiet place with grass growing through the cracks in asphalt roads that pass miles of partially abandoned military compounds. Official signs proclaim strict government security, but there doesn't appear to be much left to secure.

Here and there, entrepreneurs have gained a toehold. One of these was the Marine Placement Center, Inc. The placement in question is dead boats; it's the nautical equivalent of an automobile junkyard.

Beth and I drove through the gate in a chain-link fence to see dozens of boats—sailboats, fishing boats, power cruisers—lying haphazardly about the property, many with gaping holes in their hulls, all deteriorating in the weather, none that ever would float again.

As in other junkyards, the proprietor had removed and displayed some of the more valuable parts. The rest were still in place on the hulks, available to any customer with the necessary tools and optimism.

At junkyard prices we obtained a bathroom sink, some brass trim, and bits of rigging hardware. But a 1950s Chris Craft cabin cruiser held our prize, a genuine Wilcox

Crittenden marine toilet. True, the toilet appeared to have clogged up and stopped working several years before the death of the surrounding boat. True, some wag had painted its seat and lid bright red. But time and nature's composting had long since reduced anything actively disgusting to or-dinary dirt. The same device, new, costs more than five hundred dollars. We spent twenty.

We carted our prize home and hosed it down. The red paint came off easily enough. I disassembled the pump and rebuilt it with a kit of new valves and gaskets. Our toilet now sits in respectable serenity aboard *Anasazi*, its bowl and seat a gleaming white. You'd never know its past.

We gradually accumulated lots of other used parts: turn-buckles to tension the rigging, a dozen cleats, ten 6-inch portlights matched from three different sources, bronze chocks to guide mooring lines, brass hinges, four anchors, seven winches, shackles, snatch blocks, pad eyes, a peli-can hook, life rings, deck fill pipes, a bosun's chair, deck lights, and almost a mile of surplus rope. Sometimes we saved a little, sometimes we saved a lot. A few items turned out to be useless, but there would have been some mis-takes with new purchases, too. Overall, the money saved on used equipment certainly ran well into five figures.

⚓

Beth and I were pretty selective about the work we did on *Anasazi*. With limited time, we wanted to apply our work where, one way or another, it would have the biggest pay-off. Sometimes that payoff was in money saved, but more often it was a way to get something done just the way we wanted it, which sometimes ran contrary to efficiency, con-ventional wisdom, Chuck's advice, or all of the above.

An example. You can buy factory-made teak handrails, and any sensible, cost-conscious builder would do just that. But we didn't like the look of the off-the-shelf model; we had in mind a stronger, more graceful design. Also, Beth wanted the handrails to run continuously along the cabin top with no break, which meant that they'd each need to be 19 feet long. Call it a typical owner's idiosyncrasy.

I scarf-jointed two teak boards to make a 19-foot length, set up sawhorses in the front yard, and cut out a pair of handrails. Beth sanded and oiled them. We delivered them to Damian for installation. When he said "Nice handrails," it made my week.

Another fussy detail: I wanted to be able to catch rain on the roof of the cabin and route it into the tanks that supply us with fresh water. So I specified an inch-high molding to run continuous around the cabin top, instead of leaving the normal openings for drainage. On one Saturday visit to the shop, Beth and I climbed aboard *Anasazi* and spilled a cup of water on the plywood cabin top. The stream of water, picking up sanding dust, swirled along the cabin top to the low point. There I cut and drilled through the molding, leaving a hole shaped to funnel the water into a fitting that was measured to accept a plastic hose. Who would have the nerve to demand all that of a builder? Not I. But it was worth doing; except in a very dry climate, we cruise independent of the local water supply.

Those were small jobs; there were bigger ones. Beth designed, built, and covered every cushion on board. There are seventeen of them, and each one is curved and angled to fit its place. I built the electrical panel. Beth sewed canvas covers for the hatches and the sails. I cut the salvaged portlights down to size, and Beth cleaned and repaired them until they worked. I carefully measured and cut sixteen lengths of stainless steel cable—wire rope as thick as your little finger—and installed strong end fittings. Beth learned to splice braided line, and we made up all the sheets and halyards.

We ticked other jobs off the list as their times came: Make eighteen blocks for running rigging, make trim rings for the portlights, teak grates for the bowsprit and the cockpit, radar reflector, sun canopy, and weather cloths. Make custom chocks to hold the anchors, the life raft, and the dinghy on the cabin top. Build and install the boom gallows, install the cabin heater, wire in the running lights, splice up the lifelines and tension them into place.

One of the bigger jobs was building the metal fittings on the mast and boom: tangs to anchor the stays, hinged brackets to support the spreaders, sheaves to guide halyards, and the like. The boom fittings were bronze, but the mast fittings were to be made of stainless steel.

Working with stainless steel began as an exercise in frustration. I had no way to cut the tough stainless plate except with an abrasive wheel on the table saw. The process was slow, noisy, boring, left a rough edge, and heated up the steel to the point that I feared I was doing some sort of metallurgical damage. Then I tried to drill holes, only to have the drill bit spin ineffectually against the tough stainless steel. The cutting problem was solved quickly and cheaply by taking the pieces to be sheared at a metal shop. The drilling problem I took to Damian, who introduced me to the concepts of correct drill speeds, sharp bits, and a curious milky fluid called "water-soluble cutting oil." Returning to my drill press, I used one hand to operate the machine while the other hand dispensed the oil from a plant sprayer. It was messy, but it kept the work cool and lubricated.

Besides being cut and drilled, the stainless steel plate needed to be bent to the correct angles. I worked out a technique involving clamps, levers, and a heavy hammer. It was primitive by modern standards—in fact, it was primitive by Cro-Magnon standards—but it worked. One by one I turned out the fittings: tangs to mount on the mast and attach the stays, a swiveling gooseneck fitting to connect the boom to the mast, hinged brackets for the spreaders, with ferrules to guide the stays through the spreader tips, a bronze bail to connect the main sheet to the boom, and so forth. Later, with the mast and boom on sawhorses in our driveway, I installed all of these products. They look more industrial than yachty, but they're serviceable and strong. Every time I go up the mast I give them a casual inspection, and it gives me a bit of pleasure.

More pleasure, though, comes from items that Beth and I neither found nor made. When *Anasazi*'s construction began Caitlin and Megan were in college, and Beth and I were feeling a bit too much elbow room in the empty nest.

Some of Gary's industrial-grade metal work at the mast head. It ain't pretty, but it's strong.

Although we regarded *Anasazi* as the family boat, we knew that there was more nostalgia than reality in that thought. After all, the girls—no, Dad, they're *women* now—were far more focused on their independent futures than on their childhood experiences. To them *Anasazi* was their parents' boat, not their own.

But their independence didn't mean they were ignoring us. Caitlin learned to use a wood lathe and turned a set of hardwood belaying pins for securing the halyards. Megan used an Anasazi Indian design to make and install ceramic tiles to trim the galley.

⚓

There are few statements about sailboats that are met with universal agreement, but I believe I'm on safe ground when I venture to say that a boat ought to remain right-side-up as much of the time as possible. That's why the keel of a sailboat is weighted. Remember those inflatable plastic punching toys with weights in the bottom? When you pushed one over, it popped back up. So it is with a sailboat; the wind in the sails tends to push the boat over, but tipping the boat presents less sail to the wind. Meanwhile, the weight in the keel tends to pop the boat upright again. The two forces—the wind pushing her over and the weight popping her up—reach a balance, and the boat sails along at some acceptable angle.

Sailboats that do not have weighted keels must rely on other methods to stay upright. Catamarans and boats with unballasted centerboards get their stability from their greater width—it's easier to roll a floating log than a barge. Small racing sailboats are kept upright by human ballast in the form of athletic sailors suspending themselves out over the windward rail. It's great fun for a short bash to the finish line, but you can't live for long like that.

Historically, weighted keels are relatively new. The clipper ships did not have the benefit of ballasted keels. For all their effectiveness at fast passages, they did tend to fall over at awkward moments, with loss of life and cargo.

Anasazi's keel was to be ballasted with a lead casting weighing almost 6 tons. The lead would be fastened to her backbone with fourteen bolts of silicon bronze, each a full inch in diameter.

Pouring and machining a 6-ton casting requires unusual equipment, and it also presents a number of hazards to safety and health. Damian located a company that could do it: Mars Metal, located just outside of Toronto. Mark Fitzgerald had made a detailed drawing of the shape of the ballast. Damian lofted the drawing full size, including the positions of the bolt holes, and sent the drawing to Mars Metal.

In due time the casting was delivered by truck to a local boatyard whose 20-ton lift transferred it to a trailer. The trailer was towed to Damian's shop, and the lead casting was skidded off next to *Anasazi*. The ballast casting arrived while I was on a business trip. When I telephoned Chuck from an airport about some unrelated detail, he broke the news.

The lead ballast casting—11,700 pounds ready to be skidded into place.

"I've also been talking with Damian about that ballast problem."

"Uh, what ballast problem?"

"Oh, you haven't heard from him? Well I don't want to be the bearer of bad news, but the lead ballast arrived, and it seems that the holes were bored wrong. Damian's trying to come up with a solution, and he called me. Perhaps you'll want to give him a call."

And perhaps the Pope is Catholic. Before removing the telephone from my ear, I had reached Damian. Sure enough, the ballast from Mars was a mess. First, the holes for the keel bolts were drilled at the wrong angle. They would enter the bottom of the boat at the right place, but then they'd angle back and miss the floor timbers. Also, some of the holes came out the side of the ballast instead of the bottom. And just for an extra touch, Mars had ignored our careful design and shaped the bottom to their own curve. Maybe they thought it would look better that way.

Sure, we could ship the whole thing back and make Mars do it again, but it would cost us a month or more. With the ballast casting sitting on the shop floor, there was tremendous incentive to try to use it. It would be easy enough to fill the holes with lead, but Damian didn't know of anybody locally who could redrill them. We discussed a couple of other ideas and finally settled on beefing up the boat's floor timbers so they'd line up with new bolt holes. Damian could deal with the holes coming out the sides by notching in, installing the nuts, and puttying over the notches. The wrong curve, well, we'd just live with that.

The bad ballast casting made more work for Damian, and it left us with an installation that, although still amply strong, included excess wooden structure. But the project stayed on track.

⚓

If you're not easily shocked, then I'll let you in on a nasty secret: They're shamelessly putting aluminum masts into wooden boats these days. They're also putting sophisticated carbon fiber composite masts into wooden boats. I'd like to sniff self-righteously at these developments, but then I remember that my own wooden boat is held together with epoxy resin and sheathed with a layer of fiberglass. All right, so I do sniff just a little. But only to keep up my spirits while I'm sanding.

Chuck had been skeptical of the wooden mast from the start. "If your boat has an aluminum mast, then all I do is specify the section, and standard fittings come right off the shelf. Almost no one builds wooden masts any more, and there are no standard fittings. We'll have to design each fitting, which might come to five thousand dollars worth of engineering and design drawings. Then there's the expense of having them made. It's your boat and your decision, but I'd think this might be a good time to take advantage of current technology."

Excellent advice, but we ignored it. I took on the task of designing the mast fittings. Chuck calculated the loads they had to bear, and from there the design work was repetitious but simple. In addition to saving the design fee, I was able to draw fittings that I could build myself.

A wooden mast—62 feet of clear Douglas fir—is both strong and beautiful, and it evokes the fine feeling of all things that are both strong and beautiful. About twice a year I endure a dockside lecture from some expert who has given up a wooden mast in favor of aluminum. He informs me how much trouble wooden masts are.

I've had wooden masts for twenty-five years now, and I know exactly how much trouble they are. You give your mast a light sanding and a coat of varnish once or twice a year. You watch for dings or patches of rot, and you repair them. Every four or five years you have the mast pulled out of the boat for either a minor or major refinishing, as needed. Altogether it's more work than an aluminum mast, but it's not a terrible burden.

My next confession: Most of this work falls to Beth. We do share the routine finish work. To sand the mast, I climb into a bosun's chair. I hang the chair from the main halyard and attach suitable safety lines. Then Beth uses the big geared winch to crank the halyard, and me with it, to the top of the mast. Once I've sanded the mast and am once again walking on solid deck, Beth gets into the chair, and I crank her to the top to begin applying the varnish.

That's routine maintenance. Every few years, with the mast pulled out of the boat and resting at waist level on padded sawhorses, our equal sharing of marital responsibility goes by the boards. While Beth is scraping, sanding, and applying five coats of new varnish to the spars, I'm probably off removing a propeller shaft, or adding a hull fitting, or painting the bottom.

As reward for her efforts, Beth gets to row quietly away from *Anasazi* and admire the tall wooden spar against the spruce backdrop of a misty Maine morning. Below decks in the evening the solid mast glows with soft reflected light from an oil lamp.

The bid specification and building contract for *Anasazi* did not include the mast and boom. The reason for this omission was that not all boatbuilders also build spars.

Another reason was that the design of the spars wasn't finished in time.

It was late July 1992, two months after they were promised in the latest version of his revised schedule, when Chuck finally sent the drawings for the mast and boom. As with all the other drawings, I found lots of opportunities to nit-pick at the details. This time I was dissatisfied with the design of the masthead—Chuck's design seemed unnecessarily complex to build, and also I wanted to reduce the height of mast that extended above the sail. I was thinking about the difficulties of reaching the masthead hardware—lights, antennas, and so forth—from a bosun's chair.

We didn't get the updated drawings until September, and I still wasn't happy with the result, but I wasn't about to spend another six weeks on a revision. I took the masthead drawing to a blueprint shop for copies, then I started erasing and redrawing until I had worked out a design that was strong, didn't create construction problems, and addressed the difficulty of changing a light bulb while hanging 60 feet above the deck.

While all this was going on, it was time to select someone to build the spars. We talked with Damian and Chuck, got some quotes, and ordered the spars from Basil F. Day of Thomaston, Maine.

The family name of Day goes back some ways on the Maine coast. Basil Day was semiretired from his boatbuilding business, Georges River Boat Building and Repair. I don't know how long he'd been in the business, but his stationery was printed before the era of zip codes. He had the skill and experience, and he had the shop space and equipment. He also had access to long lengths of clear, straight Douglas fir and Sitka spruce. For Basil Day a set of wooden spars was just the right winter project.

⚓

Throughout the fall Damian's shop always buzzed with four or five projects going on at once, all destined for installation on *Anasazi*. Northeast Isuzu delivered the diesel engine. Spotless, almost glowing with fresh white paint, it looked far too big as it rested on its shipping pallet, but it magically shrunk as it was lowered onto its beds within *Anasazi*'s hull.

With the hull now upright, Hugh began work on the interior, beginning at the bow. It isn't obvious, but much of what looks like just partitions and furniture in a boat is designed to play an important structural role. The double berth that fills *Anasazi*'s forward cabin is solidly bonded to the hull as strengthening against possible collision damage. The aft wall of the head, built of inch-thick plywood, helps brace the hull against twisting strains. Working to serve both functional and structural purposes, Hugh fitted shelves and cabinet fronts into the angled, curved spaces.

Rob Robinson joined the building crew. Like almost all of Damian's employees, Rob is a generation younger than Damian. These young men bring their own skills, experience, and temperament to their work, but they also absorb a certain ethic—a level of efficiency and measure of quality—that Damian expects. In every field of endeavor there are many talented people, but only some of those people have the additional talent of inspiring the next generation. These are the teachers, and Damian is one.

Rob brought his own interest and skills to boatbuilding— he has a degree in wood technology—and he has continued to learn while working for Damian. A careful, patient carpenter, he set to work on the settees in the saloon, whose other role is to serve as tanks of drinking water.

As Beth and I visited the shop one day, Rob stopped us. "I was starting to build the pilot berth, but I wanted you to see how deep it really is. I don't know if you'd pictured getting in and out of it over that rail." We climbed below and examined the partially built structure, with pencil lines on the surrounding bulkheads showing its size and shape. As with the rest of the interior accommodation, I had made a detailed drawing of the pilot berth, but as Rob translated that drawing to the actual space in the boat, he also applied his own judgment and experience. *Anasazi* was in good hands, and I felt grateful.

Everyone had more than one project in progress. While the glue was drying in one place, attention was turned to

The diesel engine was installed before deck beams got in the way. The companionway hatch is big enough to remove the engine if necessary. At least that's what the tape measure says.

another. The crew bent deck beams over curved forms, then fitted the beams into notches cut in the structural timbers. They fashioned a sturdy step to accept the heel of the mast, bracing for the fuel tanks, framing for the hatches. With each visit to the shop Beth and I admired their progress as the carefully drawn shapes were taken from the plans and manifest in three dimensions. The bare, empty hull was becoming our boat.

All this fine progress, though, was burning money at a great rate, and once again the progress payments were exhausted before the corresponding work was done. By this time Damian knew that I wasn't simply going to open the checkbook; I would expect to make payments based at least vaguely on our contract.

"We've got a lot done, but not necessarily in exactly the order that we anticipated in the contract. So I'd like to rearrange the milestones a bit so that we can get paid for our progress."

Fine. Damian typed up a revision to the contract payment points and faxed it to me. His revision took the work from two payment points, deleted the rudder, rearranged the others items to correspond to the actual work schedule, and added a few thousand dollars.

I wanted to be reasonable, but I didn't want to be taken advantage of. We compromised by redistributing the work from the two contractual milestones over three new ones, the first of which was already complete. That made one payment due now, which was, of course, Damian's immediate goal. We deferred the rudder. The total amount paid for the work would stay the same, but there would be a small additional payment for extra materials. Damian could keep working, but I knew that we were starting to dig ourselves into a hole.

But the work hummed along. Now the fuel tanks were in, and Nat patiently fitted the galley cabinets, each plywood panel firmly supported, thinking of the day when a rough sea would send the cook careening off balance to grab whatever counter was close at hand.

While Nat, Hugh, and Rob worked inside the hull, Mike was building up the deadwood, the stacks of solid lumber that, with the lead ballast, create the shape of the keel. Next the crew fitted the plywood decking, and suddenly we could walk around on the boat.

Then, with December and cold weather approaching, Damian decided to shut the project down until March. I wasn't delighted with this idea—it meant we could forget about launching in April—but it made sense. Apparently Damian had underestimated how much *space* it would take to build *Anasazi*. Not only was she now in a larger (and uninsulated) shed, but the whole shop was filled with parts being glued up or prepared for finishing. Bending jigs occupied whole tables. Materials and supplies were stacked everywhere. Heating the entire space wasn't feasible, and the crew couldn't work without heat.

So most of the work would come to a temporary stop in mid-December. Only Nat, with some help from Damian, would continue working in a heated area of the shop, fabricating parts such as the rudder and bowsprit for installation in the spring.

With the holiday season approaching it seemed a good idea to end the year with a small celebration. We arranged a dinner at a nearby restaurant, and Damian and the rest of the crew gathered, along with wives and sweethearts. With *Anasazi* progressing nicely, the crew was feeling good about their accomplishments.

The mood was festive, and as the wine flowed it became more festive still. By the end of the evening it was determined that the "shop cruise" would be a sail on *Anasazi* to the Wooden Boat Show in late June. I saw Damian consider that date for a moment, close his eyes briefly, and say nothing. I knew what he was thinking. Every project needs a deadline, and here was a good one. Meeting it would be damned difficult. On the other hand, if the boat couldn't meet this deadline, that would mean that the project was on its way to financial disaster.

⚓

Winter is a good time to buy sails. It's the slow season for sailmakers, so it's easy for them to find time to talk. Sailmakers never have as much winter work as they'd like; a little extra business while there's snow outside is always welcome.

It used to be that building sails was just another part of building ships, and every shipyard would devote a spacious room to the purpose, upstairs above the main shop. Today sailmaking is a highly specialized craft that has evolved as a separate business, but the place where a sailmaker plies his or her trade still is called a loft.

Steve Sperry's loft is on the ground floor of a weathered wooden building on the harbor in Marion, Massachusetts. To gain entry, you pull a latch string, swing open a door of rough boards, pass under a sign that says "TODAY'S SCORE: SPERRY 4, MURPHY 2," and avoid tripping over a napping sheep dog.

Most of the first floor is open space for spreading out sails. Black industrial sewing machines are installed along two walls. Shelves along the other walls overflow with bolts of white sail cloth in various weights and finishes, colorful nylon fabric for light sails and pennants, boxes of hardware like grommets and jib clips, and the sailmaker's equivalent of what your grandmother called "notions"—waxed twine, reinforcing tape, leather chafe protectors. Any remaining wall space is covered with pictures of boats under sail. A coal-burning stove keeps it all comfortable.

After successfully negotiating the entrance passage, Beth and I shook hands with Steve Sperry. Steve is in his fifties, tall, and almost alarmingly thin. His movements are relaxed; until you see him at work on a boat you don't realize how strong and agile he is.

We had been able to find three of the sails we needed on the used market at great savings, but we would need to have the mainsail and the yankee jib built to order. We spread out *Anasazi's* sail plan.

We knew we wanted the sails made of Dacron, but we also knew that some Dacron fabric handles like roofing tin. We wanted *Anasazi's* sails to be soft so that we could furl and stow the sails easily. Steve confirmed what we feared: In their quest for faster, more durable sails, the makers of Dacron sail cloth have abandoned ease of handling as a goal, developing stiffer fabric with a hard finish. He showed us some samples, and we tried crumpling them between our fingers. They all were slippery and stiff, but some were better than others. We chose the best compromise we could.

We had arrived with a list of other specifications, and these were more easily accommodated: the locations of two sets of grommets for reefing the sail in strong winds, leather patches to reduce chafe, bronze sewn-on hanks for attaching the jib to its stay. For the mainsail we wanted no headboard and no sail battens, as these are routine causes of wear and damage. The white sails would be sewn with dark thread, so that any damage to the seams would be spotted quickly. A stitch in time.

Steve Sperry had been recommended to us by two knowledgeable people, and our impressions of him and his loft only added to our sense of confidence. Before we actually placed the order we waited for some additional samples of fabric to arrive, accepted Steve's recommendation for full-length battens in the mainsail, and dithered a bit about the cost of it all. We ordered the sails in the dead of winter, and Steve delivered them well before the last snow had melted.

⚓

Damian held out a curious object. It was a hefty bronze ring, about the size of a salad plate, with several tabs coming off it. "I had it cast at Prue, down in West Dennis. It only took me an hour to make the pattern."

Only an old boat nut would recognize the peculiar device as a crance iron. Mounted on the outer end of the bowsprit, the crance iron is the attachment point for various cables that support the sailing rig—headstay, bobstay, and whisker shrouds. It was a perfectly routine piece of marine hardware as recently as, say, 1940.

Anasazi was going to be needing quite an assortment of such specialized hardware, and Damian had found the right place to get it, a small local foundry. There are more of these foundries scattered about the country than most of us would guess, and the boatbuilders know where they are.

As work on the boat progressed Damian ordered bases for the lifeline stanchions, brackets for the rudder, and a U-shaped strap called a gammon iron to attach the bowsprit. Each part arrived the fresh brown-red color of commercial bronze, with its surface still rough from the mold.

Some of my own work on *Anasazi* also would require specialized hardware, and I was happy to find this convenient source. Making the patterns was easy: plywood, plexiglass, most any material will do. There's no requirement for strength or longevity or fine finish, just cut out the pieces and glue them together. Then fair the joints with body putty from the auto supply, and give it all a quick sanding. My kind of craftsmanship.

I quickly turned out patterns for anchor chocks, chainplates to hold the bowsprit stays, and replacement latches for a couple of portlights. Then I drove an hour "down Cape" and found Prue. The foundry is settled well into the woods in an old building that looks like a barn. Actually, all old buildings on Cape Cod look like barns, as do half of the new buildings. The next barn you see, if it isn't a gift shop, is likely to be a magnetic resonance imaging lab.

Prue's building, with a gravel floor and uninsulated walls of pine, held a somewhat greater claim on authenticity. Inside, Paul Prue took my patterns. My eyes wandered past him to the equipment for sand casting.

In sand casting the pattern is placed in a box of sand, and the sand assumes the shape of the pattern to form a mold. As with other trades, foundrymen have their own language. The box of sand, called a *flask*, has an upper half and a lower half, called the *cope* and *drag*. The surface where the two halves meet forms the *parting line*, the familiar mold line that you see on castings such as chocolate Easter bunnies.

There are limitations on the shapes that Prue can cast, because it must be possible to place the mold in the box so that the foundryman can separate the two halves of the box to remove the pattern without disturbing the molded sand. Examining that chocolate bunny, you will see that the position of the parting line is crucial; if the parting line ran around the bunny's neck, you could not have removed the pattern from the mold.

I was pretty sure that I had designed the patterns so that they could be removed from sand molds without disturbing the sand, but I asked to be sure.

"Those should work OK. We don't pour bronze too often, though. How soon do you need them?"

"No great hurry. When do you think you'll be doing them?"

"Probably in a couple of weeks. I'll give you a call when they're done."

They were done in plenty of time, the new bronze fittings met *Anasazi*'s needs perfectly, and the custom casting actually cost less than the price of equivalent parts purchased through a marine catalog. How could that be? As delivered, the castings needed to be smoothed a bit, and then any drilling of holes was my job. Hey, that's what I am here for.

⚓

We like to think that *Anasazi* has only a very basic electrical system. After all, there's no auxiliary generator, no anchor windlass, no pressurized water, no forced-air heater
or air conditioner, no TV. With a diesel engine, we don't
even have spark plugs. Of course, there *are* navigation lights,
cabin lights, bilge pumps, engine-related needs such as
starting and charging, and a few other minor items. Add it
up and it comes to fifteen or twenty electrical circuits. Perhaps we're not such Spartans after all. I set down the circuits in the specifications and drew a couple of diagrams
for the builders.

The builders of wooden boats work in a world of sawdust
and glue, strong timbers and close fitting joints—they tend
to have little patience for electrical work. For that job Damian
engaged the services of Dan Fitzpatrick.

Dan arrived equipped with all manner of small electrical
supplies and years of experience wiring boats. I met with
him to go over the specs. I thought I had covered every
detail, specified proper installation, and added a couple of
innovations of my own. Dan showed me a better way to
wire the bilge pumps and pointed out that one of my engine
circuits wouldn't work.

And he was nice about it. A specialized tradesman, Dan
could have condescended to the crew and especially to the
Owner, a semi-knowledgeable meddler who generally got
further into the details than he should have. Instead, he
joked casually with Nat as he worked. Whenever I arrived
Dan would enjoy showing me a particularly neat or clever
installation. When he finished, *Anasazi*'s electrical systems
were secure and tidy, and I had learned a good deal more
than I had expected.

⚓

If the electrical work was a lesson in successful systems,
the lesson didn't get through to the plumbing department.

Instead of bringing in a specialist, the boatbuilders tried to do the plumbing themselves. Actually, they tried *not* to do it. When Damian, who had been spending most of his days on other projects, had some time to put in on *Anasazi*, he asked Nat for an assignment. Nat, being no fool, seized the opportunity to pawn off the plumbing on Damian. Damian suddenly found other responsibilities pressing.

What exactly *is* the plumbing needed on a sailboat? Lots. In the head and the galley the sinks draw freshwater from tanks and saltwater from the ocean. The toilet is flushed with seawater, and a valve causes it to drain either over-board or into a holding tank. Then there's plumbing to empty the holding tank. There are two bilge pumps plus a manual backup. Diesel fuel from two tanks feeds the engine and the cabin heater. Seawater cools the engine, and the water thus warmed leaves the boat via the exhaust pipe. The cooking stove needs propane, the cockpit needs drains, and most everything needs vents.

All this plumbing must withstand the stresses created by vibration and the boat's constant motion. The job demands strong fittings, tight joints, and quality rubber hose that is reinforced with steel wires and layers of synthetic fabric like a radial tire. Where water plumbing connects to a hole through the hull it must be particularly invulnerable, since a leak can sink the boat. Diesel fuel and propane present their own special hazards.

The need for plumbing may have been great, but the desire was nowhere to be found. Damian eventually finished what plumbing was needed to launch the boat, and everything else was deferred. Almost all of it eventually got done somehow, with emphasis on the *somehow*. Since we've had *Anasazi* I've repaired or replumbed most of these systems. After three years I think I've just about got them right.

⚓

With the arrival of spring, Basil Day reported from Maine that the mast would soon be finished. How to transport the 62-foot varnished wooden spar the 250 miles from Maine to *Anasazi* was, of course, my problem.

I phoned a leading company in the field of boat transpor-
tation and learned that it would be a routine job. A trailer
truck and a crane truck, one day, nine hundred dollars.
Yikes!

I made another phone call, this one local. Shipherd
Densmore is one of those individuals whose given name
felicitously fits his occupation. He is the proprietor of Ship's
Rigging Service. I explained my problem to Ship.

"Sure, I can move your mast. I'll use my spar trailer and
the big pickup."

We talked about the distance, how Ship would load the
600-pound mast onto his trailer, and the cost. We were
going to save *Anasazi* half of that nine hundred dollars,
and we would have a good time doing it.

We scheduled the move on the day after I was due to
return from a business trip. I drove from the airport to the
Maine coast and met Ship early the next morning outside
Basil Day's shop. We could see our breath in the crisp air.
Basil had set the mast and boom outside on padded blocks;
in the low morning sun beads of dew sparkled on the new
varnish.

Ship had some friends living nearby, and he had asked a
couple of them to come help. Mark Fitzgerald stopped by
on his way to work at Chuck Paine's office. Each new arrival admired Basil's work. Then plenty of willing hands
horsed the mast off its blocks and up onto Ship's trailer.
Who needs a crane? Ship padded the mast and boom with
scraps of carpet and lashed everything down. We were ready
to roll.

Ship's spar trailer is a most ungainly affair to behold. Its
40-foot framework is supported in front by the bed of the
pickup truck, and in the middle on the trailer's two wheels.
The back end of the frame hangs out into space. On top of
this framework rested the spars. One end of the mast extended over the cab of the truck, and the other stuck out
behind the trailer.

Ship pulled out onto the highway, and I followed in my
car, trailing close to the red flag flapping from the end of
the mast. Although the rig was undoubtedly rugged, it flexed

Six coats of varnish the easy way. If this seems like a big job, try it with the mast vertical.

with every bump in the road. As we negotiated traffic on the beltway that skirts Boston, I ran interference to help Ship change lanes.

We arrived home in good order and were met by friends that Beth had recruited to unload the mast. "OK, everybody at once, up and over." First the boom, then the 62-foot mast rested on sawhorses in our driveway. In another month of spare-time work, we cut a tenon in the heel of the mast, reshaped the boom, applied six coats of varnish, mounted the spreaders, and installed a couple hundred pounds of hardware.

Anasazi's pieces were falling into place. There was still much to do, but the idea of launching this boat began to seem a little more real.

4

Putting Her Over-Side

Back at Damian's shop, the wide front doors were rolled open to admit the spring sunshine, and *Anasazi* had begun to look almost finished. She continued to look "almost finished" while Damian's crew worked on rub rails, bowsprit, locker doors, hatches, the galley stove, portlights, bilge pumps, deck covering, the toilet and holding tank, engine sound insulation, winch islands, and a hundred other tasks. The pace quickened. The crew abolished "Good Friday" and began working six-day weeks. I brought my work to the shop—bowsprit platform, hawse pipes, anchor chocks—and tried to stay out of the way as I installed them.

The crew worked hard and efficiently, and every day brought good progress, but the list of outstanding jobs was a tough old fighter; just when you thought you were winning it would struggle back, hit you again, and refuse to die. Then one May morning Damian phoned. "I've set a date. We're going to move the boat down to Parker's Boat Yard on Thursday, the tenth of June. We can launch that weekend."

112

I was pleased and excited, of course, but I was also impressed with Damian's decisiveness. He and I both knew full well that there was a mountain of work still to do. But he also knew that if he didn't set a deadline and a cutoff, the work would go on expanding. Ninety percent done would become ninety-five and then ninety-nine, but it never would reach one hundred.

I've been through some big projects in my life. Most of mine have involved computer software, but I think that all projects whose end is a large creation, whether you're creating a building complex, or a computer system, or a merger agreement, have much in common. There are times for contemplation, imagination, and ingenuity; there are times for deliberate craftsmanship and for journeyman hard work. There are times for celebration, and panic, and perhaps despair. And there is the time to bring your creating to an end and your efforts to fruition.

Damian scheduled the truck to transport *Anasazi*, and the crew started working toward launch day. Coamings around the cockpit, a fife rail at the mast, cabin sole, hatches, staysail traveler, propeller shaft, batteries—when you finished one job you ran, not walked, to the next. Work days lengthened. The crew was determined to make the date.

⚓

Nat had been unrelenting in his efforts to make the hull smooth and fair as coats of epoxy and primer were applied. Now the whole surface felt perfect. On the last Friday afternoon at the shop the crew turned its efforts toward the final cleanup for painting. Someone took an air hose to the rafters to blow out the dust. Someone vacuumed the deck. Someone hosed down the gravel floor. Miles of masking tape shielded the rails and fittings that were not to be painted, and piles of debris filled the dumpster. Quitting time didn't come until seven o'clock that evening, but when everyone finally left the shop *Anasazi*'s hull was ready to be painted.

Marine paint technology has come a long way since the days when each builder mixed his own white lead, linseed oil, turpentine, and pigments. Modern two-part polyurethane paints can make a hull as smooth and glossy as a black Mercedes on the showroom floor. These paints are enormously hard and durable; a good application lasts for years.

The new paints are so hard that they're not suited to traditional planked boats whose wood will normally move a bit with strain and moisture. They're perfectly suited, however, to a laminated boat like *Anasazi*. We chose a product of the U. S. Paint Company called Awlgrip.

The down side—there's always a down side—of the new paints is that they are both dangerous and difficult to apply. The instructions and warnings fill six pages. The operator dresses in a full protective suit with fresh air piped in from a compressor. According to the ambient temperature and humidity the paint is mixed from a whole chemistry set of converters, reducers, accelerators, and retarders. The paint is sprayed on to a specified thickness of 2 to 3 wet mils, allowed to partially dry, then covered with a coating of 5 wet mils. It takes a lot of knowledge and experience—what Damian calls a "PhD in Awlgrip."

Jack Erikson has the degree, and he's an artist with a spray gun. On weekdays Jack paints boats for one of the larger local yacht yards, which charges amply for his services, but Damian persuaded him to apply his talents to *Anasazi* on the weekend.

Jack arrived on Saturday morning to find the hull masked and ready, the paint and associated chemicals laid out. He mixed his brew, grumped about the lack of temperature control, donned a positive pressure breathing suit, and went to work.

It was all over by noon. The hull was a smooth, uniform tan, with a black stripe at the waterline. I could see my reflection in the deep gloss. To this day Jack will tell you exactly what went wrong with that paint job, but I could never find a flaw in it.

⚓

You don't need four-wheel drive to get to Damian's shop, but the narrow dirt road is not for the timid. Brush and small trees reach out and scrape your paint, a reminder of nature's ongoing effort to obliterate the road entirely. Three days before *Anasazi* was to leave the shop, Damian called in a tree service to prune back the foliage. The result did not appreciably increase the chances of qualifying the road for interstate highway designation, but now the cleared path was big enough to admit a boat. Barely.

Moving *Anasazi* from the shop to the water was a signal moment, and I showed up with film and camera. Our friend Pierre arrived to lend moral support, and his teenage son Fabien cruised in on his bicycle. Pierre and Fabien are veterans of my creative moving schemes. Years ago we had *Bantry Bay*'s mast lifted out by the crane at a nearby boatyard. Then at five o'clock on a Sunday morning we drove to the boatyard, levered a two-wheeled dolly under the mast, set the head of the mast in the open back door of the Toyota mini-van, and towed the mast through city streets to our front yard. Pierre served as tillerman in that operation, getting out to hand steer the dolly around the corners. At that hour not many citizens were about, but we did draw some comment as we passed the fire house. The firemen were quite understanding.

Now at Damian's shop, the truck and hydraulic adjustable trailer from Brownell Boat Works appeared right on schedule, big, blue, and brawny. The latest version of the ingenious rig that Fred Brownell invented in the 1950s, it looked like something you'd expect to find parked with its engine idling at a coffee shop along the turnpike.

Over the years, I've had a number of occasions to deal with the Brownell company. Each time it is an encounter with quality—uncompromising *quality*. Everyone—receptionists, machinists, apprentice carpenters—is helpful, competent, and effective.

And they make it look easy. Years before, when Tom Brownell undertook to drill a series of holes into *Bantry Bay*'s 5 tons of cast-iron ballast, he clamped a heavy girder drill to the tine of a forklift. Presto: a mobile, fully adjustable horizontal drill press. Nothing to it.

Naturally, the Brownell drivers are superb. This one backed his trailer, foot by foot, up that questionable dirt road, into Damian's driveway, and through the open front of the shop. As the forked trailer crept backward to surround *Anasazi*, Damian's crew removed the steel jack stands that had held the boat in place. When only two stands steadied the hull, heavy wooden sleepers were slipped through slots in the trailer beneath the keel. From his control panel the driver moved padded hydraulic arms to embrace *Anasazi*, then raised the whole bed of the trailer to lift the boat off her blocks.

If backing the empty trailer into the shop was ticklish business, extricating that trailer with a boat on it was tighter yet. No matter how he backed, filled, and cut his wheels, the driver could not quite clear the shop opening. For the moment, we were stuck. From somewhere Damian produced a chain saw and a sledgehammer, and Nat used these delicate instruments to make a slight adjustment to one wall of the shop.

With the blue tractor crawling forward in its lowest gear, *Anasazi* began to emerge from the shop. The glossy new paint on her smooth hull caught the sunlight and almost looked wet. We were witnessing a birth.

Nat, Hugh, and Rob climbed up on *Anasazi*. The driver stretched a banner across the front of the truck. In case you didn't happen to notice the 42-foot boat, you might notice this 8-foot yellow and black sign that declared a WIDE LOAD. With the crew pushing branches and overhead wires clear of the cabin top, the truck and trailer lumbered down the dirt road through the woods, across the wash, and out onto the blacktop.

With pavement under its wheels, the big truck was back on its own territory. Out in front of the truck, Damian's old gray van led our procession. Our dusty Toyota brought up the rear, and Fabien whizzed back and forth on his bicycle. We had no difficulty scattering traffic for a few miles to arrive safe and sound at Parker's Boat Yard. The whole trip may have been completely legal, but I doubt it.

⚓

After a fifteen-month gestation,
Anasazi *emerges.*

Anasazi rolled into the boatyard on Thursday afternoon, and the launch was set for Sunday at 4:00 P.M., with party to follow.

The boat was far from finished, but work now concentrated on the jobs that *had* to be done before *Anasazi* was afloat. Besides the small details, big jobs like installing the bowsprit and the chainplates to support the mast had to be completed in her three remaining days ashore.

Dawn comes early during the sunny days of June. By 6:00 A.M. on launch day Beth and I were at the boatyard installing mooring chocks so that, once launched, *Anasazi* could be tied to the dock. We were finished and out of the way by the time Damian's crew arrived at eight. I returned to my work on the rigging, and Beth went home to prepare for the launch party.

We had been keeping our family and friends apprised of *Anasazi*'s progress, most recently by the invitation to her launching that promised "Free Beer, Bad Music, Greasy Food, Old Jokes." Some well-wishers just couldn't be there. Caitlin was finishing out her teaching commitment on Guam, but we had been sending her photos of the construction, and now she sent us a congratulatory drawing. My sister in California wrote celebratory doggerel for the occasion. Megan helped Beth load up the party makings, and, despite minor injuries that Beth sustained while tying the load on the roof, they rolled up in fine style.

Sunday afternoon, at precisely 3:45, the last worker climbed down from the boat. *They finished fifteen minutes ahead of schedule!* Friends arrived by land and by boat. The whole design office—Chuck, Mark, and Maura—drove down from Maine. Damian passed out printed T-shirts identifying the *Anasazi* Building Crew. Beth hung a spray of flowers on the bow.

It was nearing high tide when Bruce Parker took up strain on the slings of his 20-ton lift, raised *Anasazi* off her blocks, and lumbered toward the water's edge. Damian donned a black tuxedo jacket over his T-shirt and shorts and perched astride the bowsprit for the ceremonial 100-yard ride to the launching slip.

With *Anasazi* suspended above the water we kept the speeches short. I paid tribute to the designers and builders. Damian saluted his crew and thanked us for having the boat built. Beth gave *Anasazi* her name; then she smashed the bottle of champagne against the new ship's bow in an explosion of foam.

Good cheer and good wishes were the order of the day as Bruce Parker lowered the gleaming hull into the lapping water of Red Brook Harbor. More from tradition than doubt, Damian climbed aboard and checked below decks for leaks. On shore there were tables of food and washtubs of drinks, and ragtime music played from hastily wired stereo speakers. The party continued into the sunset. Someone brought a fiddle. Damian averred that no launch can be complete without shrimp and champagne, and he added both.

Beth has perfect aim with the champagne bottle.

Everyone strolled aboard *Anasazi* for a look around, and the building crew was happy to show off their work. Amid the noise and merriment, Beth quietly stepped away, held her champagne glass out over the water, and tossed a splash to the Old Man. So did Damian. So did Nat.

By dusk there were just a half dozen of us relaxing in *Anasazi*'s saloon. The new cushions hid unfinished lockers, the mast and boom still rested on sawhorses ashore, and neither the engine nor the plumbing was hooked up, but at this moment none of that mattered. The biggest, most complex boat that Damian had ever built, the boat for which the building crew had worked nights and weekends, the boat that embodied dreams that Beth and I had been crystallizing ever since our family conference in the Îles du Salut, now tugged gently at her dock lines. We all gloried in the moment.

⚓

That year the Wooden Boat Show was to be held in Newport, Rhode Island, some 60 miles from where *Anasazi* now lay at the boatyard's wooden float. If we were to keep the promise of the shop cruise, we had just ten days to put *Anasazi* in commission. We were going to be spending long days at Parker's Boat Yard.

Ransom Parker, "Raz" to everyone, started up this yard after World War II. Now in his eighties, Raz Parker has turned the management of the yard over to his son, Bruce. Raz and his wife, Jean, as well as Bruce with his family, live within a few hundred yards of the launching slip. It's a family operation.

Although it's a small yard, on any given summer day you'll see three distinct groups of workers at Parker's. There are the boatyard hands hauling boats, repairing engines, tuning rigging. There are the launch and dock attendants, all female, all young and attractive in blue shorts and white sailor's blouses. And there are Raz and his retired colleagues puttering about on some project or other. There's always a friendly word, and everyone gets along.

No mast or rigging yet, but she's afloat at last.

Anasazi's interior is traditional varnished wood and light enamel.

The launch party ended Sunday night, and on Monday morning the boatyard crane lowered Anasazi's mast through the opening in the deck. We chose two coins to place, heads up, beneath the heel of the mast for good luck: one bright new penny, and one Indian-head penny that we had found in my grandfather's desk drawer after his death. Anasazi, after all, is both new and old.

With Damian's crew busily back at work on Anasazi, I scurried to attach the rigging wires to support the swaying mast. Each one of these thirteen rigging wires had been made up ahead of time with strong stainless steel end fittings. To figure out the lengths of the wires in advance, we had placed a surveyor's transit atop Anasazi's cabin roof and sighted in the chainplates. Then I took measurements from the plans and, with the help of Megan's high school math book, I worked out the length of each wire. Now with the mast dangling from the crane and the wires dangling from the mast, I hoped they would be the right length—long enough to reach the chainplates and short enough to draw tight. Most of them were.

With the mast in place I joined Damian's crew for long days of work, finishing what was needed to sail to Newport. Rob completed the interior joinerwork and installed the chainplates for the running backstays. Hugh bolted the lifeline stanchions into place and varnished the hatches. Nat installed the compass binnacle and the next phase of the plumbing. Damian hooked up the engine controls.

I finished the standing rigging, then Beth and I installed the boom gallows, cleats, lifelines, and all the running rigging, the collection of sheets, halyards, lifts, and other rope that operates a sailboat. We placed the dinghy on deck for the first time, and I fashioned wooden chocks to hold it in place.

Megan was spending her summer writing for the local newspaper and commuting to New Bedford to catch up on science courses for her pre-med requirements. Three days a week after class she would stop at the marine supply houses to pick up our current orders, dropping them off at Anasazi on her way home. The counter men got used to the afternoon arrival of the new representative of the Damian McLaughlin, Jr., Corporation, an earnest freckle-faced girl with abundant red hair.

The sails arrived, and the mainsail didn't fit. Back to Sperry for adjustment. Starting up the engine for the first time we heard a terrifying chatter from the gear box. A panicky phone call and consultation with the engine shop let us work around the problem.

The night before we were to leave for Newport we worked until ten o'clock. Then Nat and I hit the road—he for his hour's drive home, and I to the all-night supermarket for provisions.

⚓

The morning dawned hard and clear, with a strong breeze from the northwest—a fair wind for Newport. We planned to leave at 8:00 A.M.

By 9:00 A.M. we were still doing last-minute jobs. By ten we had discovered and fixed a leak in the propane lines. By eleven we were under way, motoring across the shallow harbor. On board were Beth and I, Nat, Hugh, Rob, and Rob's friend, Jessica. Our plan was to sail to Westport where we would anchor for the night. Nat's home was in Westport, and his wife, Julia, would join us for dinner aboard. Then the building crew would depart, all preferring a solid night's sleep at home to a bunk on *Anasazi*. Beth and I would sail the remaining few miles to Newport the following day.

Before actually setting sail an uncharacteristic attack of prudence made me decide to check the newly installed compass. Accordingly, we steamed about the harbor in various directions calling out bearings until the compass was pronounced satisfactory for its purpose. At last, the captain's concerns assuaged, we motored out the tortuous channel and raised sails for the first time.

Under her medium-air rig of reefed mainsail, staysail, and yankee jib, *Anasazi* heeled to the wind and plowed down Buzzards Bay at a good clip. Just how good a clip was a matter of speculation, since the knotmeter to display the boat's speed wasn't installed yet. But the day sparkled, the

The skipper takes the helm on Anasazi's
inaugural sail.

waves hissed by, and we ate up the miles toward Westport. There was no shortage of willing hands to play with the sails, and everyone took a turn at the wheel. I slipped below and soon was soundly asleep.

Westport harbor is narrow and crowded, and I was fully awake and back at the wheel to negotiate the entrance. Once inside the harbor we barely found room to anchor just outside the buoys that marked the channel. Julia arrived as planned, Beth heated up the lasagna and opened the wine, and we all celebrated *Anasazi*'s first day under sail with a festive dinner on board. After a round of farewells I rowed the crew ashore. Drowsily I returned to the boat, and Beth and I fell into our berth and slept until the sun was well above the horizon.

It was a fine morning. The sky remained perfectly clear, the wind had softened to a light breeze, the tide was out, and *Anasazi* was firmly aground.

Many yachtsmen carefully avoid ever running aground, finding the experience mortifying, even in contemplation. When the subject arises, they subtly brag about their perfect record: "Well, if I ever *did* run aground, I'd want to be certain to. . . ." Sure. Whatever.

If you travel with any sense of adventure, you will navigate rivers that wind into marshes and jungles. You will explore the upper reaches of rocky fjords. You will anchor in a bay that was last surveyed by Her Majesty's Navy in 1858. You will run aground.

With a soft sea bed and no wave action, going gently aground does no harm. You soon get over the embarrassment and dismay. It is a mild inconvenience, similar to being becalmed. With the tide rising, *Anasazi* would float off in an hour or two. Beth and I puttered about the deck contentedly in the warm morning sun.

Traveling by sailboat means living with uncertainty. The wind is fickle; the weather can turn. The cove that appeared secluded on the chart now boasts a condominium complex and shopping mall. The jib halyard gets loose and flies aloft, just as the propeller tangles in the warp of a lobster trap. Amid all of this unpredictability there is some small pleasure to be had in quietly, confidently, waiting for the rise of the tide.

In due course *Anasazi* floated free. We weighed anchor and departed Westport harbor. Now it was just Beth and me and 15 tons of sailboat. We shook the reef out of the mainsail and spread every sail we had before the light morning breeze. In the warm sunshine we sailed gently west toward Newport.

⚓

For two days we lived aboard *Anasazi* in Newport harbor, explored the show, and entertained visitors. Megan drove down to see the show, and Rob and Hugh rejoined us for the trip home.

Before we left Newport I thought it would be fun to get the knotmeter working so we could watch *Anasazi*'s performance and the effects of our sail trimming. The installation of the knotmeter had been completed except for the sensor—a plastic tube about the size of a baby bottle with a paddle wheel mounted on the end. The boat's forward motion through the water spins the paddle wheel; the spinning wheel sends speed and distance information to the display in the cockpit.

Of course, in order to work the tube must extend through the hull, with the paddle wheel in the water. The hole was there, correctly drilled before the boat was launched, fitted with a flange and securely plugged with a solid tube of the same size as the real one. All we had to do was remove the solid plug and substitute the sensor. Between those two operations we would be opening a 2-inch hole in the bottom of the boat.

There is a persistent old boating story, which I don't believe, about a man working alone who removed such a plug. The force of the incoming water blew the plug out of his hand, he fell backward, hit his head, and was knocked unconscious. The water soon filled and sank the boat, and the unfortunate protagonist was drowned. Right.

Nonetheless, I was pretty nervous about the prospect of that stream of water pouring in. We lifted the floorboards and surveyed the situation. We read the instructions twice. Then with Hugh at the ready I pulled on the solid tube, it popped out, and the gusher erupted. Hugh was right there to stuff a rag against the opening, and the flow stopped. Now get the sensor ready and do it one more time: gush, plug, and set the locking pin. We were done, we hadn't admitted more than a couple of quarts of ocean, and everyone still appeared conscious.

The weather gods favored us again with bright sun and a brisk southwest wind. Under full sail we went charging across Block Island Sound, the new meter reading a satisfying 8 knots. (All right, a speed of 8 knots does not confer bragging rights in many circles. But on a cruising boat with a 33-foot waterline, it feels damned good.) We rode the favorable tide up Vineyard Sound and into the harbor at Woods Hole, still flying the jib topsail, hoping that everyone we knew was watching.

As far as I know, nobody was. We furled the sails and caught the mooring that had been *Bantry Bay*'s for years. We had left Parker's Boat Yard and returned to Woods Hole. *Anasazi* was home.

⚓

The cruise to Newport, besides being fun, had served several purposes. It had provided a much-needed break for everyone. It had let the building crew experience the results of their dedication. It had given Beth and me another way to express our thanks to the crew. It had created a deadline, without which a boat is never finished. And it had served as the "sea trial" that was specified in the building contract.

Upon completion of the sea trial, according to the contract, we were to present Damian with a "punch list" of outstanding problems, whose correction would trigger the final payment and acceptance of the boat. I prepared a list, but it contained almost no unexpected items. There was a minor deck leak, which Rob quickly found and fixed. All of the other items were simply work that had yet to be finished. Most of the jobs were small, but there were thirty of them.

We moved *Anasazi* to the town dock, and work resumed in the July sun. Usually Nat worked doggedly alone, with occasional help from Damian or another member of the crew. Sweat was streaming from Nat's face as he forced hoses onto plumbing fittings in the stuffy spaces under the deck. Would the plumbing never end?

Unlike the cheerful efficiency that prevailed through most of the project, there was a grim, almost resentful atmosphere. There was no way to put a good face on it; Damian was losing money with every day's work.

Speed, not workmanship, was becoming the dominant priority, and some of the work was distinctly not up to Nat's usual standards, nor Damian's, nor mine. After another week the list was whittled down to four items, all minor. Damian promised to finish them soon, and I accepted the boat and wrote the last check. Sure, some of the last work had been given a lick and a promise, but it was clear that I'd be waiting a long time if I were to wait for the builder to deliver a perfect boat. The day would inevitably come when *Anasazi*'s problems would be our problems; that comes with owning a boat. I was ready for *Anasazi* to be our boat.

Besides, I didn't want to end the summer with *Anasazi* still in Woods Hole. I wanted to leave in two weeks for Nova Scotia.

⚓

I wanted to leave in two weeks, but Beth wasn't so sure. Although Damian's list was virtually done, ours was far from it. There were dozens of little jobs we had deferred along the way, which now clamored for attention. Most of the work of outfitting the boat for extended cruising remained—setting up the galley, installing the radio and safety gear, provisioning—as well as remaining details of running rigging, spare parts, and such odd items as a holder for toilet paper.

I firmly believe that never in the history of the universe (or at least not since the invention of the "To Do" list) has anyone ever cast off dock lines with every job completed. It must violate some physical law, like entropy maybe. To launch *Anasazi* on schedule we had postponed every job that didn't have to be done before she got wet. To sail to

Newport, we again put off jobs that we could sail for a few days without. Now one more time we went down the list: What really *must* be done before we leave?

Caitlin had arrived to spend part of her summer vacation sailing with us, and she pitched in to help. Beth was persuaded, we set a departure date of August 2, a couple of weeks away, and we all went back to work.

We also began sailing the boat. One Friday afternoon we put the dog on board to go for a rare family sail with our two grown daughters, anchoring in an open bay off Martha's Vineyard for the night. Innocently, someone used the toilet, flushed it, and was startled by a stream of sewage flowing from overhead. I was made aware of this development by a high-pitched scream emanating from the head.

I agreed to look into the matter. The matter in question was coming from the tank intended to hold fuel for the cabin heater, which happened to be mounted above the toilet. But that tank was still empty. Well, it wasn't exactly empty anymore, but what it contained wasn't heater fuel.

What the hell was going on? Ah, the heater tank and the sewage holding tank share a common vent. Somehow the holding tank had filled up and overflowed into its vent, and from there the sewage flowed back into the heater tank. I'll just pump out the holding tank to relieve the pressure.

I pumped, and the next high-pitched scream was mine as more sewage came down on me. Not only was I thoroughly disgusted, I was thoroughly confused. Whatever I did, I was being rained on by a stream of shit.

Did I remain calm? I did not. I filled the air with enough foul language to consign an entire church choir to eternal damnation. Wisely, Beth suggested that our daughters take the dog ashore for a walk.

I finally figured out that the toilet valve position that appeared to direct the outflow overboard actually directed it to the holding tank, and that's why the holding tank had filled and overflowed. The pump that was supposed to relieve the situation had been installed upside down, so that it pumped *into* the holding tank instead of out.

I removed and reinstalled the pump, and we cleaned up the mess. Caitlin and Megan returned with the dog. Later I plumbed separate vents for the two tanks. And survived to tell the tale.

⚓

Damian had begged off joining *Anasazi*'s inaugural sail to Newport, claiming a press of other work. A month had passed, and he still hadn't sailed the boat, so I suggested we find a time when he could go out with us.

"No, I think I'd better not. You've got to understand that *Anasazi* represents sort of a failure to me. Sure, we built a good boat, but I lost money, and now you have the boat, and I have a pile of bills. I can't claim it was anybody else's fault; I just never should have signed a contract at that price. But I wanted to get back into boatbuilding, and what it's proved is that I can't make a living at it. So you can see how sailing *Anasazi* just wouldn't be very satisfying."

It was a sobering thought. I knew that building *Anasazi* had cost more than projected, but I didn't fully recognize that the work had eaten not only the anticipated profit, but all of the cushion for overhead, and more besides.

Damian's point was this. His crew had worked efficiently from start to finish. If he had wasted time then he deserved to lose money, but with a hard-working, competent crew supported by efficient shop facilities and logistics, the cost of building *Anasazi* was as low as it could have been. If the labor had cost more than planned then the planning was wrong, but the labor wasn't wasted; its value was in the boat. In short, I had more boat than I'd paid for, and he was the loser.

While I was mulling over that thought we did manage to catch Damian in a brighter mood, and he joined us for an afternoon sail. Damian's a better sailor than I am, and he spent the afternoon scrambling about the deck, adjusting sheet leads, criticizing the cut of the sails, and making suggestions for improvements. We returned to the mooring with the glow of wind and sun on our faces, happy for the moment.

Although the contracted work was done and payments made, there were some loose ends. A few late bills and credits for returned equipment arrived. We settled all that. Then I drove up to the shop to pick up the leftover materials that, by the terms of the contract, were ours. I walked into the building that *Anasazi*'s hull had recently filled. It was swept out, empty but for the pile of leftover material in one corner—a stack of hardwood boards, some partial sheets of plywood, a plastic jug of epoxy, a few opened cans of paint, some boxes of screws. I loaded them up, and the shop was bare.

Then Beth and I asked to meet with Damian. We suggested, subject to his concurrence, that we make an additional payment for the labor in *Anasazi*. It would be spread out over several months, and it wouldn't leave him with a profit, but it would leave the project financially whole. On the morning of August 2, as we were packing up the last few items for our departure, we received a handwritten note from Damian:

> *Dear Beth and Gary,*
>
> *Many thanks are in order:*
> *Thanks for building a lovely boat.*
> *Thanks for having us do it.*
> *Thanks for being reasonable during construction.*
> *Thanks for covering the cost overrun which not only saved a financial disaster but renewed my faith in human nature.*
> *Thanks for reminding me that my heart is in the building of boats and I'm going to try to pursue it again.*
>
>

Fair Winds and Pleasant Sailing,
> *Damian*
>

That afternoon we slipped *Anasazi*'s mooring and raised sails, bound for the coast of Nova Scotia.

5

Reflections Postpartum

I must have heard it a hundred times over the course of the project: "Well, it may cost more to get a custom-designed boat, but at least you get exactly what you want." Oddly, neither premise is true. Let's start with the second point—getting exactly what you want.

The principal work of a naval architect is designing ships and boats. That statement may seem trivially obvious. If it does, then I am all the more shamed by acting as though I were completely ignorant of it. It didn't quite occur to me, at least through most of the design, that a naval architect *expects* to design the boat. Without ever quite saying so, I was trying to design the boat myself.

That is not a bad thing. I believe that an amateur who is fairly knowledgeable and energetic can make an excellent job of designing his or her own boat—or house, or work-place—with two provisos. First, the amateur must seek out the voices of experience and technical knowledge and heed those voices judiciously to fill the gaps in his own resources. Second, the amateur must recognize that the ability to design for himself is not the same as the ability to design for others, which is a very different task. (I would assert that it is the ability to design successfully for others, rather than the ability to design, that marks a professional.)

My mistake was in never admitting—to myself or to Chuck Paine—that I was trying to design the boat. If I had recognized at the outset the simple fact that the architect and I each expected to design the boat, we would have proceeded differently. Possibly Chuck would have declined such a commission. Or if he accepted it, then it would have been with the shared understanding that he was providing consultation and expertise to my design.

Since I failed to make my desire explicit, either to Chuck or myself, Chuck proceeded to take our statement of requirements and design the boat. That left me with the role of nit-picker. I had an opinion on every line, every curve, every angle, and Beth had opinions on a lot of them, too.

We inflicted a number of these opinions on Chuck. Sometimes he accepted them immediately. Sometimes he argued a position. Sometimes we compromised. I will never know how many times he shook his head in frustration and mumbled, "Why don't these people just let me do my job and design their boat?" He certainly never said it within our hearing.

You can't work with a professional, whether it is an architect or a plumber, by holding his hand and guiding his every move. Beth and I chose the battles that we felt were worth fighting. There were many design issues that we did not pursue, though, and therefore the boat that was designed was *not* exactly the boat we wanted. Perhaps that's a good thing.

A similar principle applies to construction. The builder, an experienced and committed professional, is putting his energy and thought into building the boat well and building it efficiently. If it is not evident in advance, it becomes obvious when the first board is cut: The quality of construction, including hundreds of detailed decisions, is far more dependent on the builder's own standards than on any specification.

The discretion that the builder exercises is necessary and good. Thanks to Damian and his crew, I believe that *Anasazi* is a better boat—in dozens of ways—than she would have been had my specifications been the only guide. But she is also a different boat, and here is another way in which you don't get exactly what you wanted.

Oh yes, let us not forget mistakes. Remember the ballast keel that arrived with the wrong shape? That was the biggest mistake that went uncorrected, but there were smaller ones, too. The building contract permits the Owner to demand that mistakes be corrected, but sometimes you'd be foolish to enforce that right. And no matter how careful the Owner (or even a professional representative), inevitably some mistakes will slip through undetected. Architects and owners may design and specify, but what you get is the boat that the builder builds.

⚓

Now about costs. The least expensive way to get a good cruising sailboat is to buy a used one. A competent survey will give you a reasonable assurance—not a certainty—that the boat is structurally sound. A new boat of good quality loses economic value far faster than it physically deteriorates, and the realities of the marketplace mean that you will be getting tens of thousands of dollars worth of serviceable equipment—sails, winches, electronics, engine, and all the rest—at a very substantial discount compared to replacement cost. For comparable design, quality, and equipment, you probably can't even build a boat with your own hands for the price of a sound, ten-year-old cruising sailboat.

But suppose that for whatever reason you have decided to indulge yourself in a new boat. Isn't a custom boat necessarily far more costly than a production model? In a word, no. At least it needn't be.

I kept records of *Anasazi*'s cost. Not just the bills from the architect and builder, but my own expenses for lumber and varnish, cabin lamps, and used portlights. When I picked up a couple of drill bits at the hardware store, the receipt went into the file.

Totaling the receipts and invoices took only a couple of hours, but it was almost a year after we launched *Anasazi* before I gathered the courage to reckon it all up. Back when we received the bids from builders, we estimated a total budget for the project, from design through outfitting, right down to cushions and anchor lines. The final cost was $274,000, about $5,000 over our budget.

The design fee was right on Chuck's estimate. Chuck probably did more rework than he'd allowed for, but that was offset by my providing the detailed drawings of interior cabinetwork and mast fittings.

Damian's labor overran substantially, but that was largely offset by our finding used equipment at lower cost than we had budgeted.

Had we not worked diligently and constantly to reduce cost, it would have been easy to spend a half million dollars to build a very similar boat. We received bids that were more than $125,000 higher than Damian's, and this was without even soliciting bids from the old, top-of-the-line builders. The spars and rigging (which were part of the budget but not part of the bids) could easily have cost $25,000 more than they did. New jibs instead of used ones? Add a couple of thousand. And so on, and so on.

On the other hand, this boat was not built at a rock bottom price. If you were building a boat of the same size and design, but you wanted to absolutely minimize the cost, you would eliminate the teak decks, install a good rebuilt diesel, choose a battenless main sail, eliminate some duplication in the rigging, and use a lot of stainless steel and aluminum in place of bronze. Really watching your pennies, you probably could shave $40,000 or $50,000, without changing the amount of owner-supplied labor.

Ah yes, the owner-supplied labor. For me, it made sense to keep my day job and only do for *Anasazi* what I could accomplish in my spare time. The day job suffered, but maybe not too badly. For someone else perhaps a different compromise is right. You could contract with the builder for less than a finished boat, then complete it yourself. The delusion here is that it is common knowledge (and our experience) that the hull of a cruising boat represents only about 25 to 30 percent of the time and money in her. Proceed forewarned. Alternatively, some small builders will let the owner work along with them, giving credit for hours worked. In some ways that should be great fun, not to mention educational, but it sounds like a bad idea to me. How can you be apprentice and overseer at the same time? Are you content with the lowest level, most boring jobs? What happens when you make mistakes, or make the builder's job harder, or the builder doesn't like your work? It would take extraordinary people to make that relationship work.

At the risk of stating the obvious, another way to spend less is to build a smaller boat. The cost of a boat varies roughly with displacement, so for the purpose of approximation we can say that it varies as the cube of its length. In plain language, that means that building a similar boat 36 feet long would have cost about $100,000 less, say, $175,000. (Although the radio and the galley stove aren't any smaller; better figure $200,000.)

Any way you look at it, this is not lunch money. It's not out of reach for an upper middle class family, though, if your own custom cruising boat is what you want.

Now how does all this custom work compare in price to those 42-footers at the boat show? The comparison is difficult. Those boats are fiberglass; nobody is building production boats in wood in *Anasazi*'s size range. Those boats have aluminum masts (which are fine) and hydraulically swaged stays (which are not). They have all-teak interiors (dark) and cable steering (a reliability issue), but they also have refrigerators and showers and hot running water, none of which *Anasazi* has. They have two heads and sleep eight, but there is less storage and no engine room. They are strong enough, but they are less strongly built than *Anasazi*.

Whether those production yachts represent greater or lesser value is a matter of opinion suitable for a long argument over a couple of cold ones.

The price of those boats is in the range of $200,000 to $400,000. That price passes along to the buyer the economies of amortizing the design over several hulls, plus volume procurement and production. It also passes along the costs of advertising, exhibiting at boat shows, printing glossy brochures, and compensating a force of sales and marketing people.

For Beth and me, the choice is obvious. Every boat is a thousand compromises, and I want those compromises to be mine. In everything from the size of the keel bolts to the density of foam in the cushions, our own values are built into our boat.

⚓

If a custom boat gives you the opportunity to build at least a good approximation of your dream, and if you've made your peace with the time and money issues, then what is the disadvantage? In a word, risk. This is a boat that has never been built before.

Your architect, your builder, and you are bringing your best ideas to this boat, and some of these ideas will be new ones. Whether it's an improvement you've always wanted, a clever way to design around conflicting requirements, or some structural detail as she's abuilding, innovation and originality will creep into the work of even the crustiest conservative. A boat with no innovation isn't a custom design, it's a replica. With innovation comes risk.

Anasazi floats exactly on her designed waterline. She is stiff, dry, and comfortable. For these attributes I am grateful to the architect. But not even such an accomplished and experienced architect as Chuck Paine knew with perfect certainty that the design would succeed so well.

Anasazi serves her crew's working needs well, although deck space is just a bit cramped at the bow. And she's a beautiful little ship. That's not just her crew talking; she turns heads and draws admiring comments in every harbor she enters. But don't look too closely at her transom. Alden drew a perfect oval transom; Herreshoff defined a classic elliptical heart shape, and either of these would have suited *Anasazi* superbly, but, alas, she wasn't that fortunate. Such are the risks of building hull number one.

Beth and I incorporated dozens—no, hundreds—of our own ideas into the boat. We're happy with most of them. But there are places where we were dead wrong, where we should have respected standard practice. We're paying for our audacity by replacing or correcting the ill-advised work, with innovation yielding to conventional wisdom.

Like the risk in design, there is also risk in first-time construction. In Southwest Harbor, Maine, Morris Yachts builds fast, graceful, expensive cruising boats to Chuck Paine's designs. You can watch them putting together a Morris 44. The polished hull already shines a deep Gulf Stream blue, set off by a white boot stripe. The deck, though, still lies in a different room. Inside the open hull workers are fitting systems: stove, refrigeration, bilge pump, hydraulic autopilot. The parts are installed in a set sequence, and every wire, switch, hose, and junction box has its place. The workers know exactly what they're doing, because they've done this before. Installation bugs were worked out in the first, second, and third of these boats; we're watching the twentieth. This work is superbly efficient, and the outcome is 100 percent certain.

No builder, no matter how well organized, can match that certainty and efficiency the first time he builds a particular boat. By the time he builds the fourth, he'll find a better way to reinforce the cabin top, or run a fuel hose, or sequence the work. But your boat was the first.

Does that fact excite you, or does it just make you grind your teeth with frustration? A custom boat is a gloriously complex experiment. With planning, design, and supervision, and with good people executing the experiment, the results will be very close to what you envisaged. But you can't entirely eliminate the risk of innovation. Perhaps you wouldn't want to.

⚓

So a custom boat should not—at least it need not—cost more than a comparable production boat. While you don't get precisely what you wanted, you get as close to it as possible. That much for the actual product.

The real benefit is in the process. The part you play in bringing a fine new vessel into the world—your presence at the creation—lets you meet and work with some extraordinary creators. The people who design and build boats, almost without exception, have actively chosen to learn a complex craft, then devote all their talent and skill to it, then keep learning more. It takes all that devotion to survive in the field. The dull, lazy, or marginally competent are weeded out of boatbuilding as surely as they are weeded out of brain surgery.

These capable people have chosen hard work in a field whose pay scale pulls our national average down a couple of points, and they choose it again every morning. They could get work that offers better pay and security, but boats offer allure and challenge. At the risk of overgeneralizing, I'll say that most of them make that kind of choice in other areas of their lives as well. These are interesting people to know.

And how do you, the prospective owner, fit in? Not easily. You puzzle over problems, you try to understand issues. You study books of similar yacht designs and research the engineering properties of epoxy resin, or steel cable, or Sitka spruce. You ask the advice of the people you're working with, and you seek out others to consult and kibitz.

In Costa Rica we met a fellow who had purchased locally a bare fiberglass hull and, with his own hands, built, rigged, and equipped a cruising sailboat. When asked how he had ever learned enough to complete such a complex project, he had a ready answer: "Fear." By necessity, he had used all the well-worn methods of gaining knowledge: reading, asking around, thinking problems through, making mistakes. Then he'd blundered ahead, not because he felt ready, but because he had to. It works.

During the thirty months from the start of design to the end of construction, I woke up every morning thinking about *Anasazi*. There was the design for the winch islands to draw, wire cable to order, an anchor chock to weld. There were bills to review, and a list of used sails to study. As anxious as I was to complete *Anasazi* and begin sailing her, I was sorry when the process of creation ended.

Postscript

After leaving Woods Hole on August 2, 1993, *Anasazi* spent a night at anchor in a cove up Buzzards Bay, then, with Beth, me, and Caitlin aboard, she made a direct two-day passage to Nova Scotia. She cruised Nova Scotia's eastern coast and Bras d'Or lakes for the remainder of the summer, then spent her first winter blocked up on shore in Lunenburg. The following summer we relaunched her and sailed the south coast of Newfoundland and the French islands of St. Pierre and Miquelon before returning home to Cape Cod via Nova Scotia and Maine.

Caitlin is back from Guam, living in San Francisco, teaching writing to high school students, and coaching her father through the unfamiliar task of writing a book. Megan is midway through the excitement and the drudgery of medical school.

Anasazi, launched in June 1993, has been sailing close to home, but a voyage to Bermuda and the Caribbean is on the horizon. Chuck Paine once told me that the ideal time to buy a boat is when it is three years old: nothing has worn out yet, and the owner has finally fixed most of the bugs. His maxim describes *Anasazi* perfectly.

Anasazi's design and construction is the second most interesting endeavor that I've ever undertaken. The most interesting one was raising kids. The two activities do have some common themes:

- They are best done with a partner.
- Hard as you may try, you don't completely control the process; the results show the influence of many people, and are the better for it.
- One tends to be proud, perhaps unduly proud, of the outcome.

⚓

Chuck continues his successes in yacht design. His work has been particularly well received by a growing European clientele. Very little of his work is in traditional boats; for him, *Anasazi* represented an interesting but temporary detour into his past.

Damian, after a short dry spell, has lately had all the business he can handle, building several graceful Herreshoff designs, as well as a large cruising catamaran. Nat Bryant is back working for Damian; Hugh and Rob have joined Nat from time to time. Mike is busy with his own business making signs, boat lettering, and production woodwork under computer control.

Last week the odometer on the Toyota mini-van turned past 193,000 miles. It might not stand up to the job of building another boat.

Appendix

Very few people undertake to have custom sailboats designed and built anymore. Of those who do, most have a single-minded dedication to yacht racing and are parting with astronomical sums to gain a microscopic competitive edge. Then there are a handful of huge luxury sailing yachts with seven-figure price tags. The number of ordinary, modest, capable cruising boats that are custom built each year is so small as to be almost invisible.

This doesn't make sense. Lots of people who cruise on sailboats would be fascinated by the opportunity to create the boats they want. Few of us are competent enough to build our own boat, but many, perhaps most, cruising sailors would enjoy devoting time and energy to thinking through a design, overseeing the construction, and supplementing the builder's work with a few products of their own skill and ingenuity.

This Appendix is written for those people, and for me. Its purpose is to provide the more nautical reader with more details, information, and warnings than would fit in the story.

To the extent that this is a "How To" book, well, here's how.

⚓

GENERAL DESIGN

Lines Drawings

The drawings for *Anasazi* on the following pages are reproduced courtesy of Chuck Paine. Shown last are the hull lines. Like many aspects of the boat, they represent a compromise between Chuck's expertise and our prejudice toward traditional shapes. Some quick comments:

- The full keel and counter stern were givens at the start. Chuck argued for a more vertical leading edge to improve windward ability.

- We insisted on a deadrise angle of at least 25 degrees in order to keep bilge water from flowing up into the lockers when the boat is heeled.

- Chuck's first drawing placed her maximum beam well aft, but we wanted a more symmetrical shape, largely for the traditional aesthetic, but also in hopes of improving working conditions on deck.

- If I'd had my way completely, she would have been a bit longer on the waterline, with slightly less overhang.

It certainly is possible to draw a faster boat, but *Anasazi* performs quite well, considering that other objectives took priority. Besides her traditional appearance, she is quite stiff, she has a comfortable motion, and she can carry a load. A couple of thousand pounds of cruising gear and provisions don't bother her a bit.

Anasazi's *sail plan.*

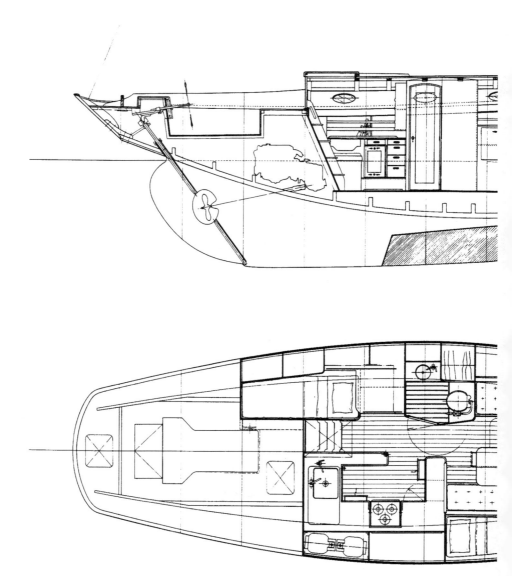

Anasazi's *arrangement plan and inboard profile.*

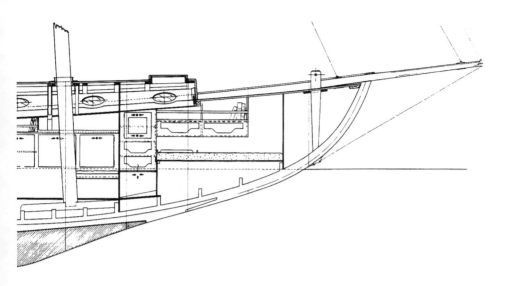

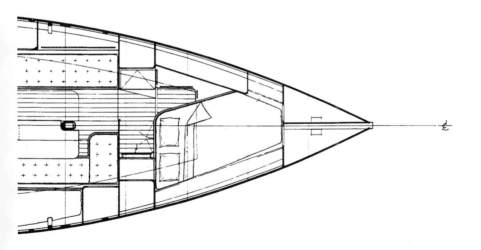

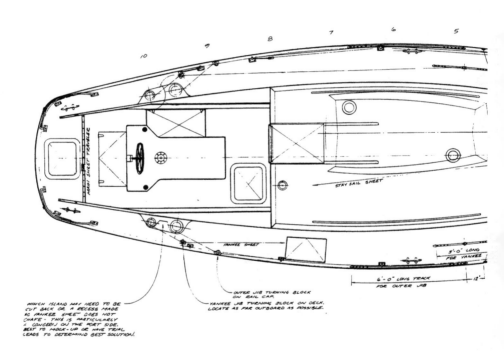

Anasazi's *deck plan*.

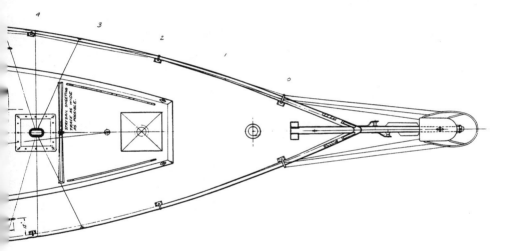

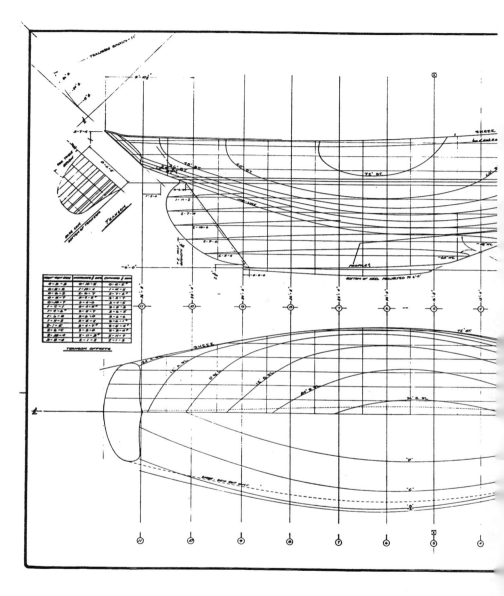

Anasazi's hull lines plan.

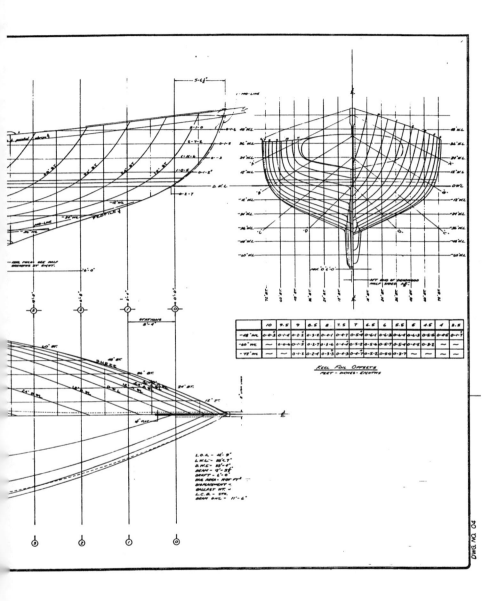

Design Work at Home

Somewhere between the architect's overall plans and the carpenter's folding rule, someone must design the details. The architect would prefer not to be bothered with this level of minutiae. The builder would prefer not to have the responsibility for design decisions. I was happy to do it, because it gave me the level of involvement and control that I wanted.

The drawings on the following pages are typical of the dozens that I made. They took at least a couple of hours each—it's amazing how much thought, reference checking, and controversy are encompassed in a few pencil lines. The more complex drawings took even longer.

In addition to providing a medium for my input to the boat, making the drawings was fun. What sailor doesn't want to add his own touches? And what a thrill to be drawing something that will be built into your boat!

For all of these drawings I made do with my poor-man's drafting equipment, but it was a struggle. Only after *Anasazi* was launched did I learn that there's a good, low-cost alternative to a true architect's drafting table. Office supply companies sell small drafting boards for around sixty dollars. You put a drafting board on a desk or table, and it gives you a smooth surface with a clip to hold your paper and built-in sliding rulers to make parallel and perpendicular lines. It's the perfect tool for the amateur draftsman.

Besides the tools, you need reference books. The best general-purpose reference on yacht design for the nonprofessional is *Skene's Elements of Yacht Design* by the late F. S. Kinney. *Skene's* covers about every subject from dimensions of the typical human through calculation of mast loading, all with a pleasant bias toward the practice of Sparkman & Stephens in the 1950s. The wealth of information in *Skene's* is presented at a comfortable level of technicality that is useful but not intimidating. Ted Brewer's *Understanding Boat Design* is worthwhile reading, although it is intended to help you to understand designs, not initiate them.

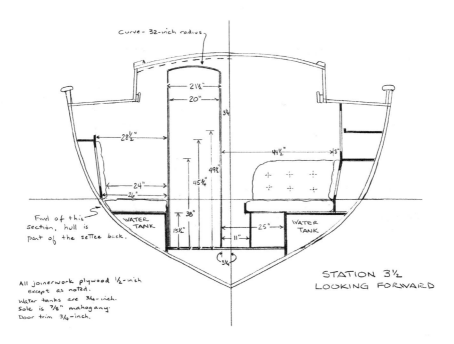

Curve - 32-inch radius

21½"
20"
¾
28½"
44½"
3"
24"
49½"
45¾"
26"
38"
Fwd of this section, hull is part of the settee back.
WATER TANK
15½"
11"
25"
WATER TANK
¾
¾

All joinerwork plywood ½-inch except as noted.
Water tanks are ¾-inch.
Sole is ⅞" mahogany.
Door trim ¾-inch.

STATION 3½
LOOKING FORWARD

The architect's arrangement plan shows the overall layout, but before the builder can cut wood he needs the height of each seat, the angle of the seat back, and the depth of each shelf. Making a drawing like this gets you thinking about just how you use lockers, and how thick the cushions will be.

Damian was emphatic: "We need the dimensions of everything. Scaling off the plans always leads to mistakes. You have the dimensions on the scale ruler while you're making the drawings, so just write them on the drawing. And try to give the dimensions from some real point you can see on the boat, not from theoretical lines like the waterline or the centerline." Here the heights are taken from the tops of the sole bearers, and horizontal distances are measured on the forward bulkhead.

For specific reference information check out *The Gougeon Brothers on Boat Construction* (wood-epoxy construction), the *Wood Handbook* (U.S. Department of Agriculture Handbook No. 72), and Dave Gerr's *Propeller Handbook*. One

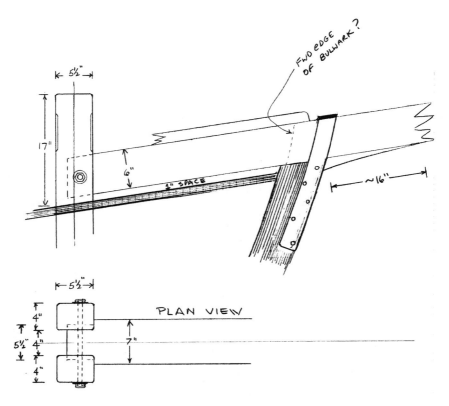

The bowsprit bears a lot of compression from the headstay,
and that compression is transferred to the mooring bitts.
Besides supporting the load from the bowsprit, stout mooring
bitts that can take several heavy lines are infinitely prefer-
able to a cleat or two. The bowsprit must be either completely sealed to the deck, or else high enough to permit
ventilation and cleaning beneath it. We chose the latter.

birthday Beth gave me *Machinery's Handbook*, a constantly-
used reference for strengths of materials, standard sizes,
etc.

Who are your favorite designers? John Alden? Philip
Rhodes? Bob Perry? Phil Bolger? Books of their designs are
useful for comparisons and ideas. And speaking of ideas,

SHROUD CHAINPLATES
ARE 29⅞" LONG

BACKSTAY CHAINPLATES
ARE 23⅞" LONG

MATERIAL ORDERED IS
TWO 120-INCH PIECES
AND ONE 48-INCH PIECE
(FOR THE BACKSTAYS)

LOWER SHROUD CHAINPLATES
TO BE BENT AS PER
"OPTION II" IN SK-08-IA.

OTHER CHAINPLATES TO BE
BENT TO ALIGN WITH STAYS.

BACKSTAYS TO HAVE
6 ⅜" BRONZE BOLTS.

SHROUDS TO HAVE
8 ⅜" BRONZE BOLTS.

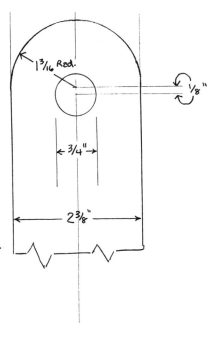

Designing chainplates might seem to be part of the black art of the architect's realm, but it's almost foolishly simple. Skene's Elements of Yacht Design shows how and gives examples.

 You start with the breaking strength of the wire that leads to the chainplate. Add a third for safety (there's already a much larger safety multiple built into the choice of the wire size). Divide by the tensile strength of the material—bronze, steel, or whatever. That gives you the cross-sectional area required in way of the clevis hole. Just pick any reasonable dimensions that give the area you need. Likewise, Skene's gives the simple calculation for the bolts needed to support the load.

you probably already have the books by Eric Hiscock, Donald Street, Ferenc Maté, Steve Dashew, Ian Nicolson, and others offering opinions, techniques, and clever wrinkles. One of my favorites is *Cruising Rigs and Rigging* by Ross Norgrove.

The Specifications

If you were to write a set of specifications for a cruising sailboat, perhaps the most useful place to start would be with a checklist of topics to be covered. To that end, the following pages provide an outline of the specifications for *Anasazi*.

I believe that this outline will serve any cruising sailboat. If you have systems that *Anasazi* does not, just add them.

1.0 GENERAL
    1.1   Principal Dimensions
    1.2   Materials
    1.2.1 General
    1.2.2 Wood
    1.2.3 Plywood
    1.2.4 Epoxy
    1.2.5 Bronze
    1.2.6 Stainless Steel
    1.2.7 Bedding Compounds
    1.3   Workmanship
    1.4   Access to Compartments
    1.5   Cleaning
    1.6   Safety Requirements
    1.7   Manuals and Instructions

2.0 HULL AND DECK CONSTRUCTION
    2.1   Hull
    2.2   Deck and Cabin
    2.3   Keel Bolts
    2.4   Bulkheads
    2.5   Bilges
    2.6   Bulwarks and Cap
    2.7   Guard Rails (Rub Rails)
    2.8   Fastenings
    2.9   Limber Holes
    2.10 Mast Step

3.0 MACHINERY

3.1   Main Engine and Gear
3.2   Engine Mounts
3.3   Exhaust System
3.4   Propeller Shaft
3.5   Shaft Installation
3.6   Propeller
3.7   Controls
3.8   Steering
3.9   Instruments
3.10 Sound Insulation

4.0 PLUMBING

4.1   General
4.2   Exhaust System
4.3   Engine Cooling System
4.4   Fuel System
4.4.1 Tanks
4.4.2 Fuel Lines
4.5   Cabin Heater
4.6   Propane
4.7   Bilge System
4.8   Potable Water System
4.9   Saltwater System
4.10 Toilet Installation
4.11 Holding Tank
4.12 Cockpit Scuppers

5.0 ELECTRICAL

5.1   General
5.2   Bonding System
5.3   Batteries
5.4   Electrical Panel
5.5   Battery Wiring
5.6   Engine Circuits
5.7   DC Circuits

Another sample set of specifications can be found in *Skene's Elements* mentioned earlier. Its author is infinitely more experienced than I, so his specifications are shorter.

CHOOSING A BUILDER

The Builder

There is another important attribute in a builder that I didn't fully recognize at the time we made the choice: complete honesty. Whatever of Damian's other strengths I appreciated, and despite whatever problems arose along the way, I always was aware of, and grateful for, his personal honesty.

The obvious first area where truthfulness is necessary is financial. Clearly, you can't work with a builder whom you suspect is overstating hours worked, or billing for extra materials that go to another job, or in some other way simply stealing.

I always reviewed Damian's invoices and backup documents. Although the review was cursory—not an audit, just a spot-check—I do have a pretty good eye for fishy numbers, and I caught a fair number of errors. Just as many of these were in my favor as in Damian's. And when Damian found an error he brought it up and corrected it, whether it helped or hurt him.

Damian's honesty, though, was not limited to refraining from committing theft. He made clear his thoughts and his reasons for them. If he wanted to change the way of doing some job in order to save time, he didn't pretend that it was for the purpose of improving the boat. This straightforward approach made it possible to discuss these issues sensibly, so it served both of us well.

Of course, I did my best to reciprocate and deal with him in the same way. So were we totally honest with each other? No, I suppose not. But when we were not totally honest, it was mostly because we also were fooling ourselves.

⚓

It should be clear that in the final analysis Beth and I were very pleased to have chosen Damian to build *Anasazi*. But what about the choice we didn't make—Tom Wostenholme? It is impossible to make the comparison. I know the strengths that Damian brought to *Anasazi*, and I know the problems that we had. If Tom had built the boat there would have been different strengths, and just as assuredly there would have been different problems. Would Tom have run a more efficient project? Or would it have been less efficient and a complete financial disaster? Would he have installed better plumbing? Would his cabin top construction have been as strong? Would he have faired the hull as well, or varnished the interior more evenly? Just naming such questions makes it obvious how pointless it is to ask them.

Anasazi could only be built by one builder, and we're delighted that it was Damian. But my contact with Tom Wostenholme left me with considerable respect for him. If you wanted to have a boat built, and traditional design was important in your thinking, I'd recommend that you have a serious talk with Tom.

The Contract—Labor Versus Materials

The form of the building contract was time-and-materials with a fixed cap on labor costs. If the labor cost came in under budget, the Builder was to keep one-third of the underrun as a bonus. Labor rates were specified in terms of actual payroll, plus fringe costs, shop overhead, and profit. The labor budget was designed to include management and clerical time. As was noted in the text, the cost of materials was left uncapped.

Several builders thought that this contract was unfair. They felt that if there was to be a fixed maximum price, then that was the price they should receive in any event, with any underrun being part of the Builder's profit. Of course, most builders simply preferred a time-and-materials contract. Who wouldn't?

As Owner I was satisfied with the form of the contract, principally because I avoided writing a blank check. Although I eventually was willing to make up for some of the Builder's cost overrun, if the contract had not been capped I would have been liable for the entire overrun, which, in all probability, would have been much greater.

One serendipitous by-product of a time-and-materials

contract, whether capped or not, is that you, the Owner, see time sheets and receipts for everything. This is an effective aid to understanding what's going on.

The big weakness of this contract was in its failure to define "materials." If the Builder buys a stern railing, that's materials. If he builds the railing, that's labor. Naturally, given no prior agreement to the contrary, he'll buy the railing. The build-or-buy decisions *should* be made on the basis of overall cost-efficiency, not on the basis of whose pocket gets hit.

If materials are to be left uncapped—which does seem sensible—then I think the contract should spell out in detail which items are to be treated as materials. The Owner and the Builder should be able to get that list about 90 percent right in advance. The rest can be changed later by mutual agreement, with corresponding cost adjustments.

Was this a fair contract? Perhaps builders feel that a capped contract is a trap. But from my perspective, a builder who gets the contract on the basis of a particular bid—and it *is* the Builder who supplied the bid—should not then be able to work merrily along, overrunning his estimate, charging it all to the Owner, and feeling no financial pain. Perhaps some "share the pain" formula would be a "fair" compromise.

CHOICES AND MORE CHOICES

Lofting—By Hand or Computer?

Anasazi's lines started out on a computer. They were completed by hand because, as mentioned in the text, Chuck felt he could do a better job on the ends of the boat than the software could. I think he also had the sense, despite all the flexibility that the computer offers, that he could get just what he wanted at the drafting board more surely than he could at the computer screen.

Even if the lines are hand drawn, they are converted to digital form in the table of offsets. The loftsman works principally from that table, not from the drawings. Is it not possible, then, to enter the offsets into a computer and let the computer produce the mold patterns directly?

It is, and Damian looked into the possibility. It would have saved several days of Nat's time in lofting, and several days of Mike's time in taking the shapes off the lofting for the two dozen molds that defined *Anasazi*'s hull. Using the computer would have required that they enter the offsets, check them carefully, and add some additional information. But even with 300 data elements, this is quicker than lofting. Then the computer plots the mold shapes onto sheets of Mylar that flow from 12-foot-wide rolls.

It takes time to do all this computer work, and dollars to rent the use of the system, but still it would have saved the project money. What it would have lost, though, is the time-honored process in which the loftsman not only checks the designer's work (what if the table of offsets had errors?) but also personally plots, sees, and gets to know each square foot of the shape. Nat wanted to start the project with that experience. It's part of the "building the boat in your head" that I think every builder needs.

Hull Laminate Schedule

Here is *Anasazi*'s hull lamination, starting from the inside of the hull:

- 5/8-inch Douglas fir strip planking, laid fore-and-aft
- 1/8-inch Douglas fir veneer, laid diagonal
- 1/8-inch Douglas fir veneer, on the other diagonal
- 1/8-inch Douglas fir veneer, on the first diagonal
- 1/4-inch mahogany planking, laid fore-and-aft
- One layer of 6-oz. fiberglass cloth

The original plan included only two of the diagonal layers, and no fiberglass sheathing. However, despite all of the successful strip-planked boats sailing the seas, I was not satisfied with the strength of that schedule.

The tensile strength of wood depends on the direction in which it is pulled relative to the direction of the grain. Pulled along the grain, wood can be enormously strong. But when pulled across the grain its tensile strength is dramatically less, typically as little as 10 percent. If you've ever split firewood, you know this to be true.

Perversely, it turns out that aligning the wood at 45 degrees to the stress does not provide the average of the two strengths. Wood under tensile stress at 45 degrees to the grain is much less than half as strong as wood pulled along the grain.

Tensile stress is exerted on hulls in many ways—by the shrouds and keel, by wave action, and by collision, for example. The stress exerted by the shrouds is vertical. The stress exerted by collision—that is, by a puncturing load—would be roughly the same in all directions. Yet the original laminate schedule left the boat relatively weak in the vertical direction, or so it seemed to me.

My proposed solution was to add a layer of Kevlar between two of the hull layers. Kevlar is the enormously strong synthetic fabric that is used to make bulletproof vests, among other things. Talk about resistance to puncture!

Chuck and Damian, in consultation with Meade Gougeon, were united in opposition to my plan. First, they felt from experience that a boat built with strip planks and diagonal veneers is very strong. Second, because Kevlar is so much less elastic than wood, they felt that there was risk that the epoxy bond between the two—inside the hull laminate—might eventually fail. The use of Kevlar in wooden boat construction is recent enough that we don't have twenty or thirty years of experience to assess the longevity of that bond.

So I was persuaded to accept a more conventional way to strengthen the hull; we added a third diagonal layer. We also sheathed the entire hull with fiberglass to form a more effective water barrier. I'm still not convinced that my plan wasn't better, particularly with respect to collision damage, but I must acknowledge that *Anasazi*'s hull has shown absolutely no sign of flexing or working in any way.

Choices of Wood

Anasazi is built principally of Douglas fir. It's a strong wood, takes glue well, is reasonably priced, and resists rot. *Bantry Bay* was planked in Douglas fir, and although her fifty-year-old oak frames suffered a good deal of rot, wherever they came in contact with the Douglas fir the hardwood was rotten but the softwood was sound. However, in my experience Douglas fir is more susceptible than other woods to chemical deterioration such as that caused by galvanic corrosion or rust in metal that is in contact with the wood.

Douglas fir is available in long lengths of good quality, even here in New England, far from its source in the Pacific Northwest. The veneers for cold molding, however, were shipped from Oregon.

Even *Anasazi*'s mast is Douglas fir. The conventional choice would have been Sitka spruce, which, being quite light, has a bit better strength-to-weight ratio, but Douglas fir's superior absolute strength and superior ability to hold screws seemed worth the added weight.

The next most-used wood in *Anasazi* is Honduran mahogany. Besides having good construction characteristics (it is only moderately strong, but it is easily machined and glues well), Honduran mahogany takes a beautiful finish. Perhaps surprisingly, it is not particularly expensive. *Anasazi*'s outer hull lamination is fore-and-aft planking of Honduran mahogany one-quarter of an inch thick. This choice was made before we decided to add the fiberglass sheathing, and it was never reconsidered. It's wasteful to use mahogany only to cover it with fiberglass, and fore-and-aft probably was the wrong direction to run it, since the innermost layer provided fore-and-aft strength and this was no longer the hull's outer surface. This misuse of the mahogany was just an unfortunate result of last-minute decision making.

Besides the hull planking, Honduran mahogany forms the caprail, hatches, interior trim, and other visually important items.

The plywood in the boat was manufactured in Israel of okoume grown in Africa. As a boatbuilding wood, okoume has the disadvantage of being relatively prone to rot, but in this high-quality plywood, which is completely sealed with epoxy, it is very strong and does not seem to pose a rot problem.

Douglas fir marine plywood is similarly strong and less expensive, but giving it a smooth finish is difficult and unduly labor intensive. We used some Douglas fir plywood where finish is not an issue, such as the upper layer of the deck, which is covered with teak.

Teak is used sparingly, in consideration of its cost and scarcity. Teak decking is a wonderful luxury that even I am willing to pay for. The other uses of teak—handrails, boom gallows, fife rail, and such—were for items exposed to the weather and difficult to keep protected. Here teak's inherent durability more than justifies its use.

I tried to avoid excessive variety in the wood species used, but different requirements kept popping up. Even with a Douglas fir mast the boom, oddly, is spruce, because here strength was no problem and the boom's weight seemed more important. There is ash veneer on the chart table, to keep it light colored. Galley counters are oiled maple, just like our kitchen at home. Blocks, cleats, and the mooring bitts, are made of locust.

In choosing woods, in particular the Douglas fir and mahogany that constitute most of the boat, I had heard that these species were available from managed, sustainable sources. I wish I could say that I then followed through and ensured that we actually procured our wood from such sources, but I did not. Damian bought it from his regular wholesale supplier. Whether that supplier attends to such matters, or whether the last spotted owl was shot to build my hull, I guiltily admit I never asked.

I now know that it is possible to learn more about sources of wood from an outfit called the Good Wood Alliance, P.O. Box 1525, Burlington, VT 05402-1525. They keep track of the work of various environmental certification agencies, and they compile lists of producers and suppliers of wood and wood products. For the cyber-inclined, they have an interesting Web site at www.web.net/~philipw/goodwood_list.

Choice of Diesel Engine

Anasazi's 60-hp Isuzu diesel engine is a bit oversized for the job; a 50-hp model would have been closer to the target. But the choice from Isuzu's product line was either 40 or 60 hp, so of course we went with the larger size.

I chose Isuzu for two principal reasons. First, Isuzu marine diesels were very highly rated in a user survey I'd read. (Isuzu is ranked first in the 1988 SSCA Equipment Survey. The 1992 survey had not yet been published when we bought the engine. In it Isuzu still gets good marks, but not as high as Yanmar and some others.)

Second, the Isuzu's physical characteristics are more reassuring. To reduce weight and cost, today's small diesels run at higher speed and higher compression than the previous generation did. Relative to other engines in its class, the Isuzu is a bit larger and heavier, and its designed compression and speed range are lower. To me, all of these characteristics sounded like reliability and longevity.

Although we've still only put a few hundred hours on *Anasazi*'s engine, I have no reason to complain about its reliability. It always starts, and it runs smoothly. There has been a lot of aggravation caused by a mediocre job of marinizing the engine: wrong belts, a misaligned pump, and an SAE oil filter that appeared to have been forced onto its metric base with a heavy hammer. There also has been a nasty gear chatter (see later section on Last-Minute Problems).

One of my favorite of the Isuzu's attributes, though, is its color. *Anasazi*'s engine is white. Relative to a red Westerbeke or a green Volvo, our white Isuzu is always easy to see as you work on it, even if you're reaching into a shadow or beneath the engine. It's easy to keep clean, because any oil or smudges are immediately spotted and are gone with a quick wipe of a rag. And if a leak were to occur from a gasket, injector seat, or whatever, that too would be quickly seen. As a contributor to the longevity of diesel engines, a light color is a much underrated factor. If the engine I wanted were dark, I would have it painted white before installation.

Steering Gear

Beth rather liked the old Edson worm gear on *Bantry Bay*. It was strong, well made, and perfectly reliable. A worm gear has a couple of disadvantages, though. It doesn't provide feedback—the "feel" of the helm—and its friction is too much for the type of small, low-power autopilot that we were considering. So we decided on a different kind of geared linkage, a rack and pinion. It's simple, strong, and time tested.

Many mechanically geared steerers are designed so that the rudder post and the steering wheel shaft must be perpendicular to each other. *Anasazi*'s rudder post is set at quite an angle, about 35 degrees from vertical. If the gear required the steering shaft to be perpendicular to the rudder post, then the steering wheel would have been placed at an awkward angle. The Lunenburg gear solves this problem with a swivel arrangement that is both flexible and very strong.

But if I were to do it again, frankly I would not buy the Lunenburg Foundry unit. It is strong, and it served the fish boats of the 1930s well, but it is too crudely built for my taste, with play in every joint. If I couldn't shake my religious aversion to cable steering, I think I'd go see the folks at Edson anyway. If one of their standard rack-and-pinion steerers wouldn't work, then they'd make up a custom model, and it would incorporate all of Edson's experience in the steering business, plus their own superb machine work.

Castlok Fittings

Stainless steel rigging wire is a boon to sailors, but ultimately the stays are only as good as the fittings on their ends. As I hope everyone knows by now, swaged wire rope terminals are a terrible idea that has been foisted on the sailing public by the charlatans of the industry. Swages are cheap (to the trade) and easy to install (if you happen to have a hydraulic rotary press the size of a small car) so they are used a great deal on factory-built production boats. But they will fail in a few years, typically developing corrosion cracks where the wire enters. Tropical sailing conditions greatly accelerate this failure.

The ideal wire rope terminal would be strong, long lasting, readily installed by the sailor, reusable, and inexpensive. Pie in the sky, you say? This device actually exists! It is the Castlok terminal produced by the Loos company, an old name in cable and rigging. The fittings work on the same principle as the old poured zinc sockets, which are still in use on elevator cables and large sailing vessels and have always been well regarded. To install the terminal, you slide the barrel of the fitting a few inches up the cable, unlay the protruding wire, slide the barrel back down over the unlayed strands, pour a special metal-filled epoxy in, and screw an eye (or jaw) into the end of the barrel. You *must* clean the wire with solvent, and there's a bit of a knack to handling the wire, but it's all well within the ability of ordinary folks.

When you want to remove a Castlok for reuse, you heat it with a small propane torch to disintegrate the epoxy, yank the fitting off the cable, clean it up with a wire brush, and it's ready to use again. I have done this. It works.

The strength of the fitting does not rely on the epoxy's adhesion, but rather on the fact that pulling the wire out of the fitting would require compressing a blob of high-strength epoxy inside the thick stainless steel barrel. I have read of the lab tests on Castloks, and they meet the obvious criterion: In each size, the installed fitting should be stronger than the wire.

I installed Castloks on *Bantry Bay*'s standing rigging in 1977. When we sold the boat in 1990, after additional time in the tropics and some hard sailing, none of the terminals showed any sign of a problem.

Ballast Casting Problems

As designed, the bottom of *Anasazi*'s keel is quite flat in cross-section. Although it may be contrary to intuition, it turns out that a flat-bottomed keel sails at least as efficiently, perhaps more so, than a rounded bottom.

The big advantage to the flat bottom is that the boat is more secure as she rests on the hard. In an American boatyard—in the world of travel lifts and steel jack stands—this is not so important. But cruising to less traveled places might mean hauling the boat on an antique marine railway, or lashing her to a bridge abutment to work at low tide, or perhaps even being stranded on a falling tide. In those circumstances I'd like my boat to have a flat keel.

In retrospect, I'm sorry I accepted the bad casting. We could have reorganized the work around that particular delay, especially considering that the project all but shut down for the winter not long thereafter. We'd have a better keel shape and a less cluttered bilge.

Electricity on Boats

Every wire connector on *Anasazi* is soldered. I've read articles by experts and I've consulted a guru or two, and no one has convinced me that there is any connection as good as solder. Of course, all wiring should be stranded and tinned; that's standard marine practice. But then they go and use those crimp connectors. Around saltwater the surfaces of both the wire and the connector will inevitably corrode. Even if the circuit still works, the corrosion has added unnecessary resistance, which matters in a low-voltage marine system. (One recent article on the subject admonished primly, "Be sure to use only good quality crimp connectors." Just exactly what *is* a "good quality" crimp connector, and how do you know one if you see it? Have you ever been offered a choice of different grades of crimp connectors? How do you know what your electrician is using? The author doesn't say.) I'll stick with solder, knowing that I need never doubt my electrical connections. In capable hands, soldering adds very little time to a whole electrical job. In my hands, well, my time is cheap.

While your soldering gun is plugged in, standardize your DC outlets. A cruising boat inevitably has a few portable 12-volt gadgets, maybe a spotlight, or a hand-held vacuum cleaner, or a removable autopilot. At first you have only a couple of them, but evidently they breed, because suddenly you realize you have several more aboard. Select one type of polarized plug and install it on all your gadgets. Then install the corresponding outlet in various convenient spots around the boat, not forgetting the engine area and somewhere handy to the cockpit. I use the Perko flat two-prong plug, but to obtain outlets I had to fashion little wooden plug-holders. You, no doubt, can find a more suitable product.

Refrigeration

Anasazi has no refrigeration, not even an icebox. This is not a choice everyone would make, but it's our choice, and it's supported by our experience of cruising for extended periods in the tropics. Boat refrigeration requires a great deal of energy, usually in the form of electricity, which must be generated at least daily by the main engine, an auxiliary generator, or perhaps a windmill or a large array of solar panels. Running an engine (either to generate electricity or to run a compressor directly) is unpleasant—why are we on a sailboat, anyway?—and the "alternative technologies" have their various drawbacks. In addition, boat refrigerators are notoriously unreliable. We've met more than a few long-distance cruising boats whose cooks have relegated the fridge to storing canned goods.

How do we manage without it? Better and more easily than you might think. We shop for fresh food when it's available, and we provision with an eye toward preservation. Cheese keeps for weeks unrefrigerated; cheesecloth moistened with vinegar retards mold. Eggs last a couple of months, although it's best to buy them fresh and unwashed, which is the only way you *can* buy them in much of the world. (Supermarket eggs have had their shells washed, which renders them permeable to the air. They're generally already a couple of weeks old when you buy them.) Potatoes, onions, cabbage, and carrots all keep well when stored in a cool locker. Dry salami is a favorite for lunch. UHT milk, available in boxes in most countries, is excellent. Beth cans chicken, turkey, beef, and pork at home. It doesn't make a roast, but it's good in various hot dishes. We're hopeless fishermen, but we often receive fresh fish as gifts or in trade. (The story of the bucket of fresh shrimp and the

Playboy magazine will wait for another time.) Canned and bottled goods such as smoked oysters, olives, relishes, salsa, and pesto sauce make nice additions. When the sun drops below the yardarm, instead of cold beer we sip a rum and lime juice in the cockpit.

Without refrigeration, what do we eat? In town, with ready access to a market, just about everything. But even when we haven't been near a town for weeks there are baked goods, rice and pasta dishes, Mexican food, omelets, and curries, as well as the old reliables like three-bean salad, tuna sandwiches, and red flannel hash. I don't know what Dinty Moore beef stew tastes like, and I'm in no hurry to find out, but one occasionally finds interesting foreign pre-pared foods that are worth the experiment. (There's a nice Scottish canned steak-and-kidney pie.)

On a shore-side walk in rural Nova Scotia we picked a quart or two of berries from bushes along the road. A few days later a friendly and thoughtful local visitor brought as a gift something we "couldn't have on a boat," a loaf of bread from the oven and a jar of home-made jam. We discreetly tucked away our own baked bread and the jam that Beth had just made from those berries.

Bilge Pumps

Bantry Bay carried three bilge pumps. Two of the three failed during our near-sinking off Brazil, and the failures are instructive.

The electric pump was the centrifugal type that is found on most boats. The particular brand was Rule, but that's not important. There's a common conception, which I shared, that centrifugal pumps can safely be run dry, be-cause, unlike the rubber impeller pump that generally is used for engine cooling water, the centrifugal pump's im-peller does not seal within its housing. No sea equals no friction and no wear on the impeller.

But these pumps apparently do need the flow of water to dissipate heat from the motor and bearings. After running dry for some time, the pump can heat up, and the plastic housings for bearings, brushes, etc., become distorted, resulting in operating failure. The moral: Avoid running even a centrifugal pump dry for more than a couple of minutes. If you accidentally do, consider the pump unreliable.

The backup pump was a big bronze manual diaphragm type. I had ordered an Edson pump, a quality name, from a mail order house. When it arrived I noted the name Edson cast into the pump. But the machining was poor, and some parts that should have been stainless steel were starting to rust. "Oh well," thought I, "another good company gone bad."

Not so. The pump's bronze driving bracket simply broke while Caitlin was pumping, and that gave us incentive, after we returned home, to investigate the matter. Turns out that Edson is still the same quality, responsible company it has always been. But its products are being "knocked off" by overseas imitators, right down to the name on the pump body. The mail order house sold us one of those cheap knock-offs as an Edson pump; I do not know whether it was aware of this substitution.

By great good fortune, when I installed the ersatz Edson I decided to leave the old Whale diaphragm pump in place as a "backup to the backup." Although it had less nominal capacity and its aluminum parts were suffering from corrosion, it was the old Whale pump that saved us. That old saw about the efficiency of a scared man with a bailing bucket may hold true for a short time in a boat with an open bilge, but bailing a cruising sailboat that way on a round-the-clock schedule would exhaust most crews all too quickly.

The best solution to our problem, of course, was to reduce the inflow. I can tell you that old-fashioned sheet lead still works wonders. Sheet lead continues to be available, at least in New England, at building supply stores in the form of roof flashing. We still carry some aboard, even on *Anasazi*. After *Bantry Bay*'s seams opened up I easily cut the lead sheet into pieces to fit, slathered them with bedding compound, and tacked them over the planking. The leakage from accessible plank seams was almost eliminated. The leakage from behind frames, floors, and butt blocks, however, could not be accessed and continued to keep us busy at the pump.

This experience also served as a memorable lesson in the disadvantage of interior ballast. In her early days *Bantry Bay* had both a cast-iron ballast keel *and* a couple of tons of internal ballast. When we bought her, the internal ballast consisted of a jumble of old sash weights, I-beam cut-offs, and rocks, in addition to iron and lead ingots, all piled in the bilge. It was a rusty, sandy mess. We threw out the rocks and the iron, cleaned the bilge, and replaced the discarded weight with more lead ingots.

Then before the Atlantic cruise we removed the ingots, had them recast, and fastened the new lead castings to the outside of the ballast keel. There are some who feel that this action caused the seams to open, but I don't believe it. After all, inside or outside, the lever arm on the keel was the same (except during the instant in which the inside ballast would shift, which is another problem entirely) because I did reduce the total weight of lead in proportion to its lower position. If the bilge had been full of ingots, gaining access to the leaks would have been, if not impossible, drastically more difficult. The same thought applies, of course, to tanks, engine, or anything else that impedes access to the bilge.

Engine Placement

The busy commercial harbor of Santo Domingo, the capital of the Dominican Republic, lies in the mouth of a river. The few visiting yachts tie to a concrete wall, always under the watch of armed guards. The guards, standing shifts around the clock, had little to do. As a courtesy we shared our meals with them. Their automatic rifles were a bit intimidating, but we got used to them.

Also tied to the wall with *Bantry Bay* was a Columbia 50 with Stu and Margie aboard. Stu was doing some plumbing work that included connections to through-hulls. At the end of the day he wrapped up the work, and we chatted as the sun went down. Beth had bought some fresh milk for our kids, and Margie offered to keep it in her fridge overnight.

Stu and Margie had not yet come on deck when we were ready to leave in the morning, so I quietly climbed aboard the Columbia 50 to retrieve our milk. I found Stu and Margie still asleep, and water rising above the cabin sole.

"Hey, Stu, your boat is sinking!" It wasn't the most thoughtful way to awaken a friend, but it worked. The problem was quickly found at one of the new plumbing joints, and Stu repaired the connection and pumped out the bilge. Although the seawater had not risen very high in the boat, it had submerged the engine which was deep in the bilge.

Picture saltwater invading the intake manifold, and cylinders, and crank case of a diesel engine. It's enough to make you resolve never to install an engine near the low point in a hull.

Paint and Varnish

Every so often *WoodenBoat* magazine has an article on varnishing. One builder applies twenty-three coats. One expert, a woman, wrote of developing your sense of *commitment* to the finish, and remarked that in order to avoid dust contamination she sometimes varnishes while nude. The thought alone is enough to give a poor skipper a palpitation of the heart. (Depending, I suppose, on the sex and inclinations of the skipper in question.)

Each time I see one of these articles, or I read instructions like "Choose a dry day with temperatures between sixty and seventy-five degrees, and avoid varnishing in direct sunlight," I want to snarl, "Get real!" Most of us, using what time we can steal, paint the topsides on an early spring day in New England, or varnish the rail while at anchor in Road Bay, or before it rains, or before winter arrives. We may bless the sun or curse it, but we live with it wherever it is. We try to outguess the weather and hope that passing trucks don't stir up too much dust.

Quite simply, there are two types of varnishing and painting: indoor and outdoor. They are almost unrelated. Boatbuilders get to do their serious finish work inside heated buildings under almost ideal conditions. The rest of us take whatever conditions we're given. This is why advice from the professionals to the amateurs often misses the point.

In choosing finish systems for *Anasazi* we tried to strike a balance between the conflicting criteria of initial application and future maintenance. Here's what we chose and why.

Most of the exterior paint, including the topside finish, is Awlgrip, a linear polyurethane. Linear polyurethanes—LPUs in the trade—are wonderfully hard and durable. As noted in the text, they are so hard that they probably are ill-suited to traditional "wet wood" boat construction. The Awlgrip brand is the industry standard, but we chose it for two specific reasons. First, using a suitable converter and reducer, it can be applied by brush as well as spray. Thus the initial application under controlled conditions was sprayed, but we've since touched up by brush. Not all LPUs can be brushed. I couldn't live with one that can't. The second reason for Awlgrip, as described in the text, is that Damian had a true expert available to apply it in the person of Jack Erikson.

Anasazi's interior paint is Pettit one-part polyurethane. It is more than adequate to the task, relatively easy to apply by spray or brush, and easy to maintain. You can touch up a bulkhead without feeling like you're reducing the life span of everyone aboard. It would be possible to Awlgrip an interior, I suppose, but it would be a counterproductive extravagance. I've used Pettit paints on a number of boats, and I think they're excellent.

The cabin top is painted with Epifanes nonskid deck paint. It's a good nonskid, but the color stability is poor. Every time I touch up the house top its color has faded, and the result is an ongoing patchwork appearance.

Varnish, of course, is trickier. When we first began to plan for *Anasazi*, I mounted a number of small squares of wood on a piece of plywood, and I applied a different clear finish to each square, using various varnishes and primers. I set them out on the shed roof of the back porch, facing south and exposed to a salt-laden prevailing wind. As a practical matter, of course, I could only test a small sample of what's available on the market. I chose Gougeon's WEST System 1000 as a proxy for all LPU varnishes, Target for the water-based polyurethanes, and Interlux 95 (Clipper Clear) for the one-parts. A friend started referring to the Schwarzman Testing Laboratory.

After more than a year the wood had weathered enough to offer some information. The WEST System 1000 proved to have the best adhesion and resistance to weathering. It is its own best primer over bare wood, just as the label says. It fared less well when the wood was coated with epoxy.

The Interlux 95 did a pretty good job. The Target suffered badly from the ultraviolet exposure. Contrary to its advertising, I don't believe that water-based polyurethane is a credible exterior coating, at least in as many coats as I'm willing to apply.

We used WEST System 1000 on *Anasazi*'s brightwork. It proved to be even tougher than expected, standing up to a lot of foot traffic and even abuse from anchor chain. It was not as resistant to UV light as we expected. Although the UV didn't damage the varnish, the varnish allowed the UV to penetrate and discolor the underlying wood.

LPU varnish isn't easy to use, requiring a strong solvent that smells dangerous. It's a two-part mix, so what you don't use is wasted, and we're talking about stuff that makes single-malt Scotch look cheap. One of its parts has a limited shelf-life—about a year depending on ambient humidity and how well you can keep it sealed. Once applied, LPU varnish is sensitive to moisture—even damp air—for a long time after it has dried to the touch. When a fog rolled in unexpectedly, Beth's careful varnish job turned a milky white!

All this is partly moot because Gougeon no longer markets WEST System 1000, but I believe that similar concerns apply to other LPU varnishes. So we've decided—Beth has decided; this is her department—to give up the toughness of LPU varnish in favor of the superior UV protection and ease of use offered by one-part varnish. Our current favorites are Epifanes and Z-Spar Flagship, but check back with us in a couple of years.

A worthwhile source of information on varnishes—maybe a better one—is *Practical Sailor* magazine. They conduct multiyear tests that are summarized in each year's April issue.

Standing Rigging

My philosophy of standing rigging is pretty simple: It must be strong and reliable, it must be owner-maintainable, and it must be designed so that no single rigging failure will result in the loss of the mast.

To accomplish the no-single-point-of-failure goal, *Anasazi* has four shrouds on each side: uppers, intermediates, and a pair of lowers, with each shroud leading to its own chainplate. She also has two standing backstays. There are no link plates joining two stays into one anywhere.

The wire itself is the usual 1 × 19 stainless steel, sized per Chuck Paine's conservative calculations. The wire terminals—the Castloks described earlier—are amply strong and not subject to the stress failures of swages. They can be removed and installed without special equipment by ordinary mortals. And they're priced far more reasonably than the extravagantly expensive Norseman and Sta-Lok fittings.

We have some bronze turnbuckles on the backstays and inner forestay, but the heavy lifting is done by the 3/4-inch galvanized steel turnbuckles on the headstay and all the 3/8-inch shrouds. I do not trust stainless steel turnbuckles at all, although I make a grudging exception for the vastly oversized one on *Anasazi*'s bobstay. Yachtsmen sniff at my galvanized steel turnbuckles, but they are far stronger than bronze at a third the cost. Grease 'em, cover the threads, and paint 'em black. They look quite shippy.

Last-Minute Problems

Apparently it's quite common: The designer measures the mast drawing and specifies a length for the sail luff. In *Anasazi*'s case that was 50 feet, 3 inches. The sailmaker dutifully builds the sail to that size. No one allows space for a fitting to connect the halyard to the sail, or for any stretch in the luff. The result: The sail is too big, and you can't tension the luff.

Steve Sperry didn't even grumble much. He just cut the head of the sail back 10 inches or so, and the sail fits fine, although the shape of the head, on inspection, is a little surprising. Moral: If achieving that last hundredth of a knot isn't your highest priority, order any sail that is intended to fill a stay or spar to be built a few inches shorter than the designer specified. It's the safe side.

⚓

It was several days after the launch that Damian finished hooking up the engine. We poured a jerry can of fuel into the tank and fired her up. Sounded good. Then we ran the shift lever into the forward position, and a godawful hammering sound made us quickly shift back to neutral. A little experimentation showed that the hammering stopped at higher speeds, say, above 1,200 rpm.

The Isuzu folks insisted that it wasn't hurting anything; we could use the engine while we tried to solve the problem. That meant spending as little time as possible in gear at low speed, but that was no big deal.

Considerable additional research revealed that the problem was not in the gearbox, but in the engine. Gear chatter is a known, common problem with small Isuzu diesels (although the dealer would never acknowledge that fact, I heard it from several engineers and mechanics). Evidently there is an imbalance in the engine that shakes the gearbox.

It took two years of persistent nagging and listening to creative excuses, but I finally succeeded in getting the dealer to supply and install a damper plate in the linkage between the engine and the transmission. The problem was solved, but be warned.

FINAL CONSIDERATIONS

Optional Extras

Here's where I make the confession: After the boat was launched, and outside of the budget, we did add a few items. Satellite navigation in the form of GPS was still in its infancy. All the satellites weren't up yet, and the price was twice what it would be a couple of years later, but I bought one. Now, who can live without GPS? I also added a simple car radio and tape player, and an 800-watt inverter in or-der to be able to operate power tools on board.

Later, before we sailed to Newfoundland, I mounted a radar antenna on the mast and plugged in a small liquid-crystal radar, the Raytheon RL-9. With the coasts of both Nova Scotia and Newfoundland buried under a blanket of fog for days at a time, I'm glad I did. We entered harbors that would have been impossible to navigate without radar, sometimes seeing the opening in the cliffs just as we en-tered, sometimes well after we were inside. Call me a wimp, but navigating by the sound of breaking surf is something I'm content to read about.

Where modern conveniences are concerned, that's about it. We still cruise happily without a VCR, or a Cuisinart, or a fridge. I'm thinking of bringing a very small icebox aboard; it'll be pleasant to have when ice is particularly convenient, but we're not depending on it, and we're not about to get involved with mechanical refrigeration.

Cost Comparison

A good production cruising boat for comparison with *Anasazi* is the Royal Passport 41. At 41 feet, 8 inches, it's a foot shorter on deck than *Anasazi*, but it also is a few inches wider and a bit longer on the waterline, so we can call the boats the same size. The Royal Passport's designer, Bob Perry, is well known and respected. Although the boat is built in Taiwan, it is sufficiently well constructed to have earned a Boat of the Year designation from *Cruising World* magazine. It's no gold-plater, but it appears to be a solid boat.

The "sailaway" price of the Passport 41 was $287,000 in 1996. That includes only the working sails and fairly mini-mal equipment—adding the rest is up to the owner—but all that equipment is brand new, which is more than *Anasazi* can boast.

To cruise the coast or most of the world with four or five people, one could choose a Royal Passport 41, spend an-other $20,000 and two or three months getting ready, and take off. Or, for the same money and a lot more time and effort, it is possible to cast off the dock lines of a custom-designed, professionally built cruising sailboat. The price is the same; the choice is yours.

Design Risk

If I were building the second *Anasazi*—or any other boat— I would pay more attention to drainage. Although all reasonable angles of heel must be considered, the biggest problem occurs with the boat lying quietly at her mooring. The rule is simple, but we somehow missed it: Any place that can possibly accumulate water not only must be drained, it must slope at least 2 or 3 degrees toward the drain. A slight slope is not enough, because there will always be small changes to the boat's trim caused by the state of the tanks, stowage, etc.

Anasazi's cockpit benches are practically level where they meet the coaming. Likewise, the bottom of the propane locker is exactly parallel to the waterline plane. (Chuck originally drew the cockpit sole as level, too, but fortunately we caught that one and corrected it.) With a near-level surface, you may drill an additional drain at today's low point, but tomorrow when you fill a fuel tank the low point moves, and you have a puddle again. It was a mistake, and it's difficult to correct now. Fortunately it's only an inconvenience.

Index

Other titles of interest

How to Design a Boat
John Teale

John Teale takes the reader step-by-step through the stages of designing both power and sailing boats, while also explaining the reasons behind the process. A very practical book that will enable even the first-time designer to produce a worthwhile boat design.

How to Paint Your Boat
Nigel Clegg

This book answers all the boatowner's questions, explaining in non-technical terms correct surface preparation, dealing with defects, correct application methods and gives advice on storage times and estimating quantities. There is even a fault finding chart when things go wrong.

Surveying Small Craft
Ian Nicolson

"...not merely a diagnostic reference for surveyors... should be required reading for designers and builders as well.... enables the average owner to become sufficiently well versed in the subject as to efficiently hold his surveyor accountable to a high standard." *Professional Boatbuilder*

Cold-Moulded and Strip-Planked Wood Boatbuilding
Ian Nicolson

This book is a practical guide to both methods, starting from the design requirements, necessary tools and working conditions, and choice of timber through step-by-step construction and repair.

Boat Data Book
Ian Nicolson

This essential technical handbook is full of details and specifications for boat construction, repair, and equipment, given in a series of easy-to-read tables and diagrams. The standard reference work for boat designers, builders, surveyors and anyone interested in repairing, refitting, and maintaining powerboats and sailboats.

Sheridan House
America's Favorite Sailing Books

Other titles of interest

Advice to the Sealorn
by Herb Payson

"Payson covers a broad range of cruising topics in an informative and often entertaining manner. Whether planning to extend your cruises or live aboard, this is good reading." *Cruising World*

Sails Full and By
Dom Degnon

A light hearted tale of a circumnavigation aboard a 41-foot ketch. Colorful places and people encountered, from the crew to the locals. "...a grass-roots adventure in the tradition of Mark Twain and a pleasing read." *SAIL*

The Long Way
Bernard Moitessier

This is the incredible story of Moitessier's participation in the first Golden Globe Race. For seven months, the veteran seafarer battled storms, doldrums, gear failure, overwhelming fatigue and loneliness. Then, nearing the finish, Moitessier pulled out of the race and sailed on for another three months before ending his 37,455-mile journey in Tahiti. Not once had he touched land.

The Incredible Voyage
Tristan Jones

During an intrepid six-year voyage to become the first man to sail on the highest and lowest bodies of water in the world—Lake Titicaca in the Andes and the Dead Sea in Israel—Tristan Jones dodged snipers, fought off starvation and travelled a distance equal to twice the circumference of the world.

By Way of the Wind
Jim Moore

Jim and Molly Moore quit their jobs, abandon their middle class lifestyle, build their own boat, and sail around the world. A fascinating and hilarious tale of a memorable voyage. "The best sailboat cruising book to come out in a long time ." *Washington Post*

Sheridan House
America's Favorite Sailing Books